THE MARKET IN BABIES

THE MARKET IN BABIES

STORIES OF AUSTRALIAN ADOPTION

Marian Quartly, Shurlee Swain, Denise Cuthbert

With Kay Dreyfus and Margaret Taft

 MONASH University Publishing

Monash University Publishing
Building 4, Monash University
Clayton, Victoria 3800, Australia
www.publishing.monash.edu

Monash University Publishing brings to the world publications which advance the
best traditions of humane and enlightened thought.

Monash University Publishing titles pass through a rigorous process of
independent peer review.

www.publishing.monash.edu/books/mb-9781921867866.html

Series: Australian History

Design: Les Thomas

Cover photograph © Marcin Smolarek / 123RF.

Frontispiece © Jan Kashin, *The Warrior Princess* (2004). Reproduced with permission
of the artist.

National Library of Australia Cataloguing-in-Publication entry:

Author:	Quartly, Marian, author.
Title:	The market in babies : stories of Australian adoption / Marian Quartly, Shurlee Swain and Denise Cuthbert.
ISBN:	9781921867866 (paperback)
Subjects:	Adoption--Australia--History.
	Intercountry adoption--Australia--History.
	Interracial adoption--Australia--History.
	Wrongful adoption--Australia--History.
	Australia--Social conditions.
Other Authors/Contributors:	
	Swain, Shurlee, author. Cuthbert, Denise, author.
Dewey Number:	362.7340994

Printed in Australia by Griffin Press an Accredited ISO AS/NZS 14001:2004
Environmental Management System printer.

FSC
www.fsc.org
MIX
Paper from
responsible sources
FSC® C009448

The paper this book is printed on is certified against the Forest
Stewardship Council ® Standards. Griffin Press holds FSC chain
of custody certification SGS-COC-005088. FSC promotes
environmentally responsible, socially beneficial and economically viable
management of the world's forests.

TABLE OF CONTENTS

LIST OF ABBREVIATIONS
AND ACRONYMS

AAFA	Australian Adoptive Families Association
AASW	Australian Association of Social Workers
ABC	Australian Broadcasting Corporation
AICAN	Australian Intercountry Adoption Network
ALAS	Adoption. Loss. Adult. Support.
ALMA	Adoption Liberation Movement of Australia
ALRC	Adoption Legislation Review Committee [Victoria]
ARMS	Australian Relinquishing Mothers Sisterhood; also Association of Relinquishing Mothers; also Association Representing Mothers Separated from their Children by Adoption
ASIAC	Australian Society for Intercountry Aid (Children)
AVI	Adopted Vietnamese International
CSMC	Council of Single Mothers and their Children
ICSW	International Council on Social Welfare
RAP	Rights for Adoptive Parents
SLRC	Statute Law Revision Committee [Victoria]
VANISH	Victorian Adoption Network for Information and Self-Help

LIST OF ILLUSTRATIONS

A NOTE ON THE AUTHORS

Marian Quartly holds the position of Professor Emerita at Monash University's School of Philosophical, Historical and International Studies. She has published for many years in the area of Australian history, with special reference to the history of the family and gender relations. Her current research concerns are the history of women's activism and the history of family in late twentieth century Australia.

Shurlee Swain is a Professor at the Australian Catholic University. She has published widely in the history of women and children, with a particular interest in the impact of welfare on individual lives. Her publications in this area include *Single Mothers and Their Children: Disposal, Punishment and Survival in Australia* (1996), *Confronting Cruelty* (2002), *Child, Nation, Race and Empire* (2010), and *Born in Hope: A History of the Early Years of the Family Court of Australia* (2012). Currently Professor Swain is the historian chief investigator on the National Find & Connect Web Resource project.

Denise Cuthbert is currently Dean of the School of Graduate Research at RMIT. She has a long-standing interest in adoption and family formation and has published on the experiences of non-Aboriginal women who adopted and fostered Aboriginal children. In her recent work on the history of adoption in Australia, Denise has published widely on the politics and philosophy of adoption policy. In 2009 she co-edited with Ceridwen Spark *Other People's Children: Adoption in Australia* (Melbourne: Scholarly Publishing).

A NOTE ON THE USE OF TERMS

The language of adoption is a fiercely contested area. Mothers separated from their children by adoption reject all the terms that have been used to describe them: biological mother, relinquishing mother, natural mother, birth mother. They want to be known only as mothers; anything else denies the reality of their relationship to the children they bore.

Women who adopted children complain in their turn about being called adoptive mothers. They feel that they have been mothers to those children in the fullest possible sense, and that the term adoptive mother diminishes them.

Adoptees are indignant when they are referred to as children. They are mostly adults, well on in years, and determined to be in charge of their own lives.

In writing this book we have not used these offensive terms, except in cases where we are directly quoting the words of our historical actors. We apologise if this causes any distress to our readers.

ACKNOWLEDGEMENTS

This book is the summation of five years of research, and we have had a lot of help along the way. The Australian Research Council provided the Discovery Grant that has been the project's life-blood. The Academy of the Social Sciences in Australia gave support for a workshop on the policy implications of our research.

Kate Murphy, Kathy Lothian, Nell Musgrove, Margaret Taft and Kay Dreyfus have all given invaluable assistance as research fellows. Amy Pollard's PhD research has enlightened us about the movement for adoption reform. A number of people have helped us with particular projects, both as researchers and as organisers; these have included Jill Cox, Ana Kailis, Sally Newman, Sarah Pinto, Ceridwen Spark, and Sam Cavarra and his team from the Victorian Department of Human Services. Our work has also been enriched by collaborations and assistance from other adoption researchers, including Karen Balcom, Joshua Forkert, Patricia Fronek, Jessica Walton and Indigo Willing. Oral historians who have collected adoption stories for us include Jeannine Baker, Patricia Curthoys, Karen Downing, Rosemary Francis, Jennifer Hamilton-McKenzie, Naomi Parry, Pauline Payne, and Dominic Golding who did all the interviews of intercountry adoptees.

Building and maintaining the History of Adoption website has involved the efforts of a wide range of IT experts from Monash University. We thank especially Anthony Beitz and Nicholas McPhee from the Monash e-Research Centre, and Joanne Sullivan from the Arts Online Presence Team, without whom the project could not have been carried through. Keeping the project ticking over financially was made possible through the efforts of Tommy Fung and Alice Davies at Monash. At ACU our thanks go to colleagues in the School of Arts and Sciences (Victoria), and in particular to Sylvia Herlihy, whose quiet efficiency ensured that this collaborative project went smoothly.

Many participants in the history of Australian adoption have shared memories and documents with us, too many to name. Our understanding has been immeasurably enriched by their willingness to provide information, to answer queries and to critique our work.

Above all we are grateful to the storytellers, named and unnamed, who posted their stories on our website. This book is dedicated to them.

INTRODUCTION

Adoption is a subject that divides public opinion. People take strong positions that leave no room for debate. Some agree with celebrity Deborra-Lee Furness that adoption is a legitimate way to form a family, and the best way to relieve the sufferings of the more than '100 million orphans in our world'. Others hold that adoption is a crime against mothers and their children that can never be justified.

Fifty years ago the Furness position was generally accepted within Australian society. Social workers, psychologists, health professionals, ministers of religion, editors of women's magazines, all agreed that adoption was the perfect solution to two social problems. Couples who couldn't have children could solve their infertility problem by adopting a baby to rear as if it was their own. And young mothers could escape the shame of an illegitimate baby and get on with their lives. Infertile couples strongly supported this way of thinking, and parents of young mothers tended to agree. Mothers and babies were not consulted; it was assumed that their elders knew best.

Today this position is under challenge. The self-help groups formed in the 1980s and 90s by mothers separated from their children have brought the pain of separation into public view. They have won the ear of politicians. The Prime Minister has apologised on behalf of the nation to parents and children separated by adoption for the pain caused them by past adoption practices. Most of the state parliaments and religious institutions administering adoption have done the same.

The significance of adoption within Australian society has also changed. Fifty years ago adoption was an unspoken secret within many Australian families. Thousands of children, mostly babies, were adopted every year. In the ten years after 1968 about 68,000 children changed hands. Today the situation is very different, with only a few hundred adoptions a year. Adoption is history to most young Australians, history that they do not understand.

This book sets out to tell the history of adoption as it has been experienced by those involved. You will find here the voices of people separated by adoption, and of those who have chosen to adopt. In telling these stories we consider why people took the decisions that they did—how they understood their situation and how much choice they had.

As historians we also have our own story to tell. It is a story that goes beyond the understanding of particular actors, to look at the forces that have moved them. We find that a market in children has long existed in Australia, shaped by supply and demand: the demand of those seeking to adopt, and the supply of babies available for adoption. Our story turns on the changing interaction of these forces, and the efforts of social workers and politicians to control the market. It is a complicated story, and before immersing the reader in its detail we offer here a survey of its major turning points.

*

Adoption in its broadest sense is the transfer of a child from their birth family into the care of another. Adoption in this sense has been practised for as long as people have lived in Australia. Aboriginal families have always taken in children in need of care, and the same can be said about the early years of white settlement. Grandmothers often took in their sons' and daughters' children and raised them, sometimes as their own. In the absence of grandparents, friends and neighbours of needy children often did the same.

The market in children came into play as city populations grew. Here the exchange of children was between strangers. This is first visible in the classified advertisement columns of the metropolitan newspapers. From the 1840s these carried advertisements from people wanting to adopt and from parents unable to keep their children. It was always a buyers' market, with more children available than places for them. 'Sellers' often offered a cash payment to cover the costs of the adopting family.

These were private arrangements, not authorised by law. It was not until the 1920s that legislation was passed in all states establishing and regulating adoption as a legal practice. From this time all adoptions had to be registered, giving the adopted child a new legal identity as a member of her adopted family. The exchange of money was made illegal. The introduction of legal adoption dampened but did not eliminate the trade in children.

The acts were intended to encourage adoption by giving new parents security of possession, and preventing contact with the birth family. The response was not great; no more than a few hundred children a year were adopted in each state across the 1930s. Demand for adoptable children took off suddenly during the Second World War. In 1942 the balance of buyers and sellers advertising in the papers shifted decisively, with more people wanting children than there were children available. Intending parents also wanted more security of possession. State parliaments responded by passing a series of laws which sealed the original birth records and cut off all contact with the birth family.

The adoption laws of the 1950s and 1960s also reflected the influence of the new profession of social work. Social work and legal adoption practice grew alongside each other. The new adoption laws authorised social workers to decide which couples were fit to adopt, and which babies were fit for adoption. Social workers remember these years as a time when the profession found perfect homes for perfect babies. But in retrospect it is clear that the market was driven by the demands of adopting parents. On the supply side, single mothers came under great pressure to give up their children for adoption.

Adoptions peaked in 1971–72, with 9,798 children adopted across the country. From that peak numbers dropped sharply and suddenly. By 1975 they had fallen to about 5,000 a year. After that the decline slowed, but the total has not topped 1,000 since 1991. This collapse of the domestic market has been caused by a decline in supply; children are no longer readily available for adoption. The rapid decline in the 1970s reflected the fact that women with unwanted pregnancies suddenly had options other than adoption. Contraception and abortion made it easier to escape pregnancy in the first place. New Commonwealth social security benefits were introduced for single mothers in 1973, supporting and validating their choice to keep their children. In the longer timeframe more women were in the workforce, and childcare was becoming cheaper and easier to find. By the 1980s mothers and their grown up children were publicly challenging the worth of adoption, and social workers began assisting young mothers to keep their babies.

Demand from prospective parents has not declined alongside supply; people unable to bear their own children have turned to other ways of making families. In-vitro fertilisation has produced miracle babies for thousands of couples since the 1980s, and disappointed thousands more. A growing market in overseas adoption attracted Australians from the late 1970s, with numbers peaking at about 400 a year in the late 1980s. During the 1990s overseas adoptions equalled and then exceeded the declining totals for the domestic market. Most Australian states amended their laws during this period to open sealed adoption records and to allow contact between the families involved; this move towards open adoption probably also encouraged intending adopters to look overseas.

Now total adoptions have declined to less than 500 a year. About half of these are children adopted from overseas. Approaching a third are 'known child' adoptions, by foster-parents, step-parents or other family members. Babies and toddlers born in Australia and adopted by strangers make up less than 10 per cent of all adoptions today. Intercountry adoption is also in decline, with major suppliers withdrawing from the market. Intending parents are turning to a new source of supply—the global surrogacy market. Estimates suggest that in 2011 more than 200 Australians paid to have babies grown in the unregulated Indian market. Adoption as a way of making families seems to have a limited future.

Part I

EXPERIENCE

CHAPTER 1

BEING ADOPTED

Barry John Ford knows how to tell a good story. His account of his adoption begins at a moment of high drama.

> In 1992 I was in Concord Hospital, with my wife, sitting on a chair next to my mother who was dying. She had Alzheimer's for a long time and just before she died she asked me why I was sitting with her? I replied that she was my mother, who I loved, so where else would I be?

> Her response was that I was not her son but the son of a younger woman who had other children and that I was adopted. I was 46 years old at the time. I told Mum that she was the only mum I had ever known, and that as such I was not interested in the other woman. Mum died that night.

Barry comments that his Mum's confession was not a great surprise. He knew that his mother had had some fifteen miscarriages before having him. And he knew that he looked and felt nothing like the rest of the family.[1]

> As a young adult I did not drink beer, smoke, know what horse/dog won the last race and did not have a great deal of interest in football, all of which made me a bit of an outsider at any family function.

Still, he was a bit annoyed to find out that he was the only one not in on the secret.

> A few years ago I attended the funeral of my father's sister and asked my eldest cousin if she was aware of my adoption; she replied that everybody in the family knew but me, I was not impressed.

---

1   Stories in Chapter 1 are drawn from the Monash History of Adoption website: http://artsonline.monash.edu.au/historyofadoption/

Barry was adopted in 1946. Laws had been in place since the 1920s requiring all adoptions to be registered, and social workers were beginning to be involved in organising adoptions. But Barry's adoption was more in the old style, done in the way that adoptions had been arranged from the nineteenth century and earlier. His first mother and father lived and worked close to the sister of the woman who adopted him; both wives worked in a spinning mill and both husbands worked with racehorses. The adoption was a private arrangement between families, made when Barry was six months old and only registered legally six months later.

Seven years after the death of his adopted Mum, Barry set off to find his other family. He describes this as a search for identity, for himself and for his family.

> In 1999 I decided, after a long discussion with my wife, that for our own family's sake it was time to try to establish just who I was. I had put it off for so long as I did not wish to dishonour the memory of my parents.

The family he found was not a happy one. His parents had married in a hurry; his mother was only fifteen years old, his father twenty four; 'they were married in June and I was born in November'. The decision to adopt out seems to have been taken by his maternal grandmother. Two other children born over the next few years were both placed in an orphanage in about 1952.

Barry has no doubt that although he didn't fit in his adopted family, his adoption was a success.

> My adopted parents did at all times what they considered to be the best for me... My only complaint about my adopted parents is that they both drank too much, then argued, and they both smoked. All in all, very little to complain about.

He has established 'a warm relationship' with his birth brother; 'We talk every week and visit at least once a year'. His sense of loss focuses on his flesh and blood relatives.

> My biggest regret is that for some 54 years I believed I was an only child only to find that I have both a half sister and brother... I missed out on growing up with them, but by the same token I would most likely not have had the upbringing and benefits I have enjoyed and could have ended up in the orphanage with them.

Barry is nothing if not pragmatic.

BACKGROUND

This chapter is based on stories that people have contributed to our project website http://artsonline.monash.edu.au/historyofadoption/. We asked people with experience of adoption to tell us their stories. Some people gave their story in writing, others told it to an oral historian. About forty five of the stories are from people who were adopted.

People have been legally adopting babies and children—taking them into their homes as their own kith and kin—for more than a hundred years in Australia. Adoption laws were first passed in Western Australia in 1896, and in all the other states during the 1920s. Adoption happened long before there were laws about it. In rural communities families with a child they could not keep would give it to another family where its labour would be useful. In the growing cities of Australia, women placed classified advertisements in the daily papers seeking to place children in a good home, or offering to take them in. These children were not exactly for sale, but money certainly changed hands; those taking in children expected some recompense.

Making adoption legal did not lead immediately to a large increase in the numbers of children adopted, but by the 1940s there was a growing demand from infertile couples for children and especially for young babies. By the 1950s supply was also increasing, as more young, single women fell pregnant, and their families turned to adoption as the only way to hide what was thought of as their shame. Numbers rose rapidly in the 1960s, and in 1971 there were almost 10,000 adoptions. From that peak the numbers fell dramatically, halving by 1975, and declining steadily thereafter. We will discuss the reasons for this later in the book. For now it is enough to note that community ideas about the shame of illegitimacy changed, and mothers were able to keep their babies.

The forty-five stories on our website cover most of the span of adoption history: the earliest adoption was in the 1930s, the latest in the 1980s, and the stories come from all states of Australia. But there is good reason to suspect that our sample does not represent the full range of opinions about adoption. It is likely that many people who have been adopted had no interest in contributing to our website: because their adoptions were unimportant in their sense of themselves, or because they preferred not to think about adoption at all. We cannot tell these people's stories here. Our story tellers are all vitally interested in the fact of their adoption, and in its often traumatic impact on their lives.

SECRETS

The legal act of adoption requires the extinguishing of one legal identity with its associated set of family relationships, and its replacement by another. It was not until the 1990s that governments began to encourage 'open adoption', in which ties to the birth family are not lost. So adoption has long been about concealing the past, about creating secrets. From at least the 1940s, some of those who adopted tried to keep that knowledge from their children. While Barry's discovery of his adoption on his mother's deathbed is more dramatic than most, discoveries late in life are not uncommon amongst our storytellers.

Most people were shocked by this discovery. Maree Thorpe tells how

> Mum died 1994, and in November 1995 Dad moved into Aged Care, my brother… and I were cleaning out Dad's garage where we laughed at old pay dockets, newspapers etc. I came across adoption papers dated 1950 I thought Mum had tried to adopt a child before I was born. Wrong—they were my papers!
>
> I was in shock, my brother just held me—after, he told me he'd had to promise never to tell me of my adoption… My husband and I were the only ones who didn't know of my adoption…

A storyteller who prefers to remain anonymous writes that

> I never knew, never had a clue and found out by accident when I was 38. It slipped out during a conversation with an aunty. I was devastated, angry, confused, wanted to abuse everyone in the family. They all assumed that I knew and the subject was never brought up… The day I found out, my Father had already passed and my Mother was in a nursing home with dementia, so she couldn't answer any questions. I suffered and had a mild nervous breakdown.

For Annette Schlafrig, the discovery changed her life forever.

> My entire world was torn apart once I opened that letter and nothing would be the same again… my life was crumbling and everything I believed in from childhood was questionable and shaky.

Annette's sister didn't get on with their mother and always hoped that she was adopted. When the law changed in New South Wales to allow adoptees access to their original birth certificates, her sister applied and urged Annette to do so as well. She told Annette that the new birth certificates issued to children when they were adopted carried a clue: 'if there was a gap in the date of your birth on your birth certificate and the actual date you were registered with the State it could indicate you were adopted'.

Annette did not want this knowledge, but could not resist it.

> After putting down the phone I couldn't resist looking for my birth certificate. I charged up the twenty stairs to our bedroom and began rummaging through the drawers. The first certificate I came across was my husband David's, he was registered three weeks after his birth. Next I found our boys and knew they had been registered within a few weeks.

> Finally I stared down at my birth certificate in utter astonishment as the date SEPTEMBER 1955 jumped out of from the page at me. I had to look again to confirm it. I was, after all, born in March. There was a gap of six months.

Her sister was 'in raptures' to discover that she was adopted, but Annette had felt much closer to her adopted parents.

> Disbelief that I had been lied to for my entire life was the over-whelming emotion that penetrated my being. It was increasingly difficult to comprehend what I had done to Mum and Dad to deserve this betrayal of my love and loyalty. I felt discarded and abandoned by the very people whom I had relied upon and believed my entire life.

Like Maree Thorpe, Annette was also appalled to discover that her terrible secret was a secret only to her and her sister: 'all my peers and even my husband and his sister had known that [my sister] and I were adopted'. Annette has put the pieces of her life together again, but relations with the parents who adopted her have never been the same.

Carol Meckan's story tells us about secrets and half-secrets, truths and half-truths. Carol was adopted in a country town in 1947. Her mother told her that she was adopted when she was about seven years old. Carol reports that she was thrilled, and raced off to school to tell everyone, only to find they did not believe her. When she asked for corroborating evidence, her mother clammed up and refused to say another word. 'Ask me no questions', she said, 'and I'll tell you no lies'.

Carol was left with a truth that concealed more secrets than it revealed. This did not trouble her at the time; she remembers the talk of her mother's friends as full of secrets.

> There were all sorts of secrets in our town. Older women suddenly had babies—nobody commented, and you sort-of knew what was happening—as you got older you knew what was going on, and you were never shocked by anything.

Other children found the knowledge of their adoption was a heavy burden. One anonymous storyteller reports that when his sister told him the truth—at about thirteen years old—

> There was high drama in the house that night. I vaguely remember my adopted mother telling me and asking me if there was anything I wanted to know, but I was too embarrassed and just wanted to crawl away and hide.

> Over the coming years, my adoption was rarely mentioned, apart from being told that 'I was special, I was chosen'. I never believed this due to feelings of being so different from my adopted family (why would they 'choose' someone who is different).

And this difference carried a sense of shame. The mother who gave birth to him, he was told, was 'a woman of low morals'. Small wonder that when his adopted mother offered to tell him more:

> 'No, no', I remember saying in alarm—yet inside I did want to know who she was, but this seemed to me as being so disloyal to my adoptive mum.

> I spent many hours daydreaming about my mother, and why she had given me up—I really wanted to know all about her and the adoption, but could not ask my family as it seemed both a 'taboo' topic and seemed disloyal to me.

From the 1940s social workers routinely advised adopting parents to 'tell' their children the truth at an early age, and this is reflected in the pages of popular women's magazines of the time. It seems that many did not heed this advice, fearing to destroy the feeling of belonging between child and parent.

Annette's story shows how painful it could be to lose this sense of belonging late in life. But for those who 'knew', the bare fact of being adopted could also be a burden. It remained secret knowledge, not to be shared. Another anonymous storyteller who was adopted during the 1970s writes that

> In my generation it was rare to have anything about adoption validated or normalised, anything that related to my deeper feelings anyway. It was all pushed away, not spoken about, the message from my family and society is 'let's pretend that you are not adopted', which means shutting down all feelings about what and whom has been lost.

THE LOST MOTHER

The search for the lost mother is central to many of the stories. One anonymous contributor begins his story with the long letter that he wrote introducing himself to his mother in the hope that she would want to meet him.

> I feel compelled to write this letter now, today, as I am experiencing an emotional stage after receiving the paperwork relevant to my adoption. I have discovered a lot of information I was unaware about just a few months ago, and I am glad I made the decision to finally enquire about the connection between you and me and wish I had done it long before now. The reason I hadn't, was because I have always been concerned I may put you in an uncomfortable situation should I send you a letter like this, it still does concern me, but I feel it important that you hear from me, and to let you know that I am doing OK, and my life right now has turned out fantastic. I hope you can say the same.

He has often thought about his mother, and hopes that she has thought of him.

> I'm sure you must wonder from time to time about my life, and the path I have ventured down to get me where I am right now. I know I have often thought about where you are and how you are getting on, I have my entire life. Especially on my birthday, and times I have been really happy or sad, and sometimes just out of the blue.

His adoption was not a happy one.

> I don't believe I had a good childhood, I was abused both physically and emotionally... and when I look back as an adult now, I feel many of their actions were grossly inappropriate from a couple that had taken the steps and actions they did to adopt 2 children. At times I was belittled by them for being adopted, at times I was kicked, punched, slapped, scratched had things thrown at me, told I was hated and assured I would be kicked out of home as soon as I reached 18.

But he assures his mother that he doesn't believe she is in any way responsible for what has happened to him; rather he is telling her these things 'so as you can get an understanding of how I grew up and became the responsible, caring adult and parent that I am today, I think and hope you would be proud'.

There is a lot of anxiety in the letter. It revolves around an unspoken fear: that his mother will not respond. He tries to forestall any fears she may have. He worries that

> birth mothers commonly believe they have done something wrong in relinquishing a child, many feel guilty for years, some their whole lives, this is one of the main reasons birth mothers don't tend to want to make contact again with their adopted child. Many birth mothers do not want to have to experience the pain of their adopted child negatively questioning why they were given up, stirring old emotions and putting them in a position of embarrassment.

This, he assures her, is something he would never do. He assures her that 'most adoptees feel the way I do, with a great appreciation and connection with the person that give birth to them than she could ever imagine'.

He concludes with an appeal that surely no-one could resist.

> I have tried to make this introduction special, as you are so special to me.
> I look forward to hearing from you very soon.

As it happened his mother responded immediately, and contact between them has been good.

Other storytellers share this contradictory desire for contact and fear of rejection. Another anonymous story teller whose mother refused to see him wondered whether he could go through with it himself if she changed her mind.

There is so much anxiety within me about this. I know it is an irrational thought, but I still ask myself why my mother gave me up, did she just not like me, did she know I was going to be a problem child? And then I do judge her in thinking that contrary to the statue I have put her on, that she is not all that nice as 'what mother would not agree to meet her child'—and then I think, that whilst I think I am an OK person, maybe as I am from my mum, that maybe I am not such a nice person as I think.

Others tell more positive stories. An anonymous storyteller tells of her journey across the continent to Perth to meet the mother she has never known. 'There is no word', she writes, 'to describe the meeting between a mother and a daughter who have never met'. The meeting is easy, but they remain strangers. When they come to part

> I once more look into the eyes of this woman: connected by blood but a stranger to me. We share the same nose but the character in her face tells a story I don't know.

But the conclusion is positive; 'the arteries of the past' have been opened, and 'new stories [can] flow through'.

Sue Bond's story also comes to a positive conclusion. It has elements of pain like many of those discussed here—of pain and of secrets.

> I became depressed and developed anxiety whilst at university, attempting suicide in the second year. This was hidden, and I spoke to no-one about it for years. My parents did not do anything about my obvious distress, and neither did I. Our house was full of secrets.

When she decided to search, she found her mother quickly.

> Before the reunion with my birth-mother, we spoke on the phone. She wept, saying she had been afraid I would reject her because she had given me away. It had never occurred to me to be angry towards her, because I had no idea what her circumstances had been. Like many women who were pregnant and unmarried in the past, she did not have a lot of choices. But she had hoped, right up until I was born, that somehow she could keep me.

> When my dearest friend drove me up to the little country town where my birth-mother lives, I rang as we got close so she knew to look out for us. We overshot the driveway, but came back and turned in. The

image of my birth-mother standing under the carport, waiting for me after thirty-seven years, is one that I will never forget. I think of her face as emanating light.

IDENTITY

Barry John Ford began his search for his mother 'to try to establish just who I was'. Nearly all the story tellers are on this same journey, but they look for different signposts. Those whose adoptions date from the 1950s and 1960s often talk about a search for identity, though this means different things to different people.

Christine Kowal's search for identity is understood in a number of different ways. She was born in a regional city in 1956, the child of Dutch parents who had been Japanese prisoners of war. Her parents' marriage ended four months after she was born, and two older children became part of a new family with their mother. Christine was adopted at the age of eight months by an English couple living in Melbourne who were unable to have children.

> I am told that when they brought me home… I used to sit in my cot and rock incessantly. Sometimes I would push myself to the end of the cot and bang my head against it incessantly. It took many weeks to get me to cuddle in response to being held. Instead, I used to push away and stare.
>
> Gradually, my new parents and grandparents won me round until I became a confident and rather precocious child.

Christine was told the fact of her adoption when she was seven, and accepted it happily. 'After that no-one made mention of it, and it was as if I was my parents' natural child'. From the age of fifteen she began to wonder about 'what might have been the circumstances of my birth', but out of respect for her parents' feelings

> I put my curiosity aside even after I had looked in the mirror for the umpteenth time and thought, 'Who are you, really?' For me, therefore, there was a new dimension to the usual experience of 'a teenage identity crisis'.

Other storytellers report similar experiences in front of a mirror. One writes that

[Adoption] was a 'thing' I carried with me and its importance ebbed and flowed. My strongest memories of 'its' importance are looking in the mirror at my hair colour, my nose, my freckles—all features that distinguished me from my 'family' and wondering where they had come from, who they belonged to and what it would be like to look at someone with the same features.

Christine married and had two children, without feeling any need to search for further information. When a letter came from her first mother, seeking contact, Christine was angry. A change in the adoption laws had opened her private life 'to the scrutiny of some government-sanctioned body that knew more about me than I did, and I resented it'. She replied refusing contact.

It was not until another decade had passed that Christine finally agreed to contact with her birth family. She has not found the process easy: 'At times it has been joyous and at others, unbelievably difficult'. Her adopted parents were initially hostile to her making contact: 'in referring to their parenting of me they used harsh words like "charade" and "forty years' babysitting"'. Her birth family tended to assume a too-ready ownership. Christine struggled to explain to her birth sister

how devastating it was to believe you were one person and then find yourself shaken to bits then reassembled as someone else. That's how the experience of adoption and reunion seemed to me.

Her solution turned on the imagined—and entirely real—congruence between legal identity and personal identity. Christine had never sought out her original birth documents; now she saw the need to do this.

I rang the Adoption Agency, explained my situation, and they assembled the relevant paperwork. At an interview, I received each document pertaining to my former identity and circumstance and was able to take home a complete dossier, to look at in my own time, rather than rely on the information I had been given by my birth relatives. For the first time, I was struck by the amount of information I could see on my original birth certificate alone. There was my birth name, my place of birth, my sibling's names, my parents' marriage details, and even the address of my grandparents. With this, and all the other documents, I silenced all the rumours and speculation that I'd heard in both families or dreamt up myself. It somehow empowered me to be in possession of my own 'facts'. It was the beginning of coming to terms with the new person I'd begun to build.

Other storytellers also collapse the distinction between legal identity—the person described in official papers—and sense of personal identity. Suzanne Lowe found her mother in a retirement home, with only months to live. When she died Suzanne was the only living relative, and was landed with the task of cleaning out her room—

> which was hard but [I am] so grateful as this is how I found out my identity a bit as some records were there as she had applied for the birth parents' information from adoptive services. I spent days going through this. It was exciting but also depressing.

One anonymous storyteller began searching as a teenager, at a time when birth records were still closed. She fantasised that she had Aboriginal ancestry: 'I think it was my way of identifying with "the other", "the marginalized"'. She was disappointed to discover from her adopted mother that her birth parents were New Zealanders. As soon as she turned 18 she applied to the government for non-identifying information about her birth family. She received it, and

> That was it, there was nothing more that I could do. The law allowed no more. And so for the next seven years I continued as I had, carrying my adoption with me as that something extra, but this time, with some knowledge, albeit little, of my true self.

ETHNIC HERITAGE

Ethnic difference is not an issue for most of the storytellers. Aboriginal ancestry could be a welcome discovery. Maree Thorpe found some 'interesting' information on her 'birth Dad':

> His life wasn't great and his story isn't pretty. I've read records of arrests, prison, escape... I have learnt that is where I get my determination and tenacity from, and various other traits—and I thank him for that. I have come to accept him for what he was and times were very different then. I visit his grave from time to time. I found he had Aboriginal Heritage and strangely that didn't surprise me at all, somewhere deep inside I always sort of knew that (sounds odd, I know).

But for seven of the story tellers, ethnicity is central to their experience of adoption. All were born in Asia: four in Vietnam, two in Malaysia and one in Nepal. All arrived in Australia during the 1970s.

From the 1970s Australian couples who were unable to have children began adopting children from overseas. An important cause was the failure of supply in the domestic market. The first groups of intercountry adoptees came from Vietnam, 'rescued' by Australian volunteers from the horrors of what the Vietnamese call 'the American War'. The media attention given to these 'waifs' encouraged childless couples to look to other war-torn countries like Cambodia, bringing an increasing flow of babies to Australia. The storytellers on our website were amongst the earliest of these intercountry adoptees.

The experiences of these storytellers are similar in some ways to the stories told by people born and adopted in Australia, but in other ways they are very different. Jen Fitzpatrick starts her story by telling her interviewer that 'I've always known I was adopted, because I'm Asian and my parents are, you know, Caucasian. It's quite obvious'. That fact made all the difference.

Adoption was never a secret in Jen's life. From as soon as she can remember her parents told her stories about her adoption. Her mum told her how her mother had lovingly left her on the doorstep of the orphanage in Saigon, where she would be safe. Her dad's favourite story was about visiting Jen in the orphanage—how she had sat and stared at these white strangers—'Who the hell are they?'—and only came to him when he paid attention to another child.

Her new parents had had two miscarriages, and were very keen to adopt a child from Vietnam. They had put themselves through all the bureaucratic hoops required by adoption agencies in Victoria, including 'deliberately becoming Christians'.

Jen was classed as a special needs child. She was born with a cleft palate, so she was undernourished and her health was really bad. She left Vietnam in the first mass airlift of babies to Australia in April 1975, hurried away while Saigon was falling to the enemy, with scores of babies packed two by two in cardboard boxes on the floor of a cargo plane.

She grew up in country towns in Victoria and later Queensland, at a time when the nation was making the difficult transition from White Australia to multiculturalism. For most of her school days she was the only Asian child in her class, the only Asian her schoolmates had ever seen. They made racial comments, sometimes abusive ones. Her dad was abused for being with her in the street. Her parents tried to help her to deal with this. Her mother tended to get emotional, which didn't help. Her dad always said 'It could be worse'; 'Chin up and deal with it'; and while at the time this was hard, Jen believes it was good advice. She learned to deal with difficult things by herself.

Jen grew up without any sense of being Vietnamese; 'I was only Vietnamese when I looked in the mirror'. Her parents tried to fill the gap, driving her long distances for Vietnamese language classes, but she felt inadequate there, and uncomfortable. Vietnam for her was clouded by the war, which left her with a sense of pain and sadness. The first time she felt that she belonged as a Vietnamese-Australian was at university, where she met Asian students who accepted her for what she was, without any expectations or questions. For the first time she did not have to be 'an open book' for strangers to read as they felt inclined.

She did not go back to Vietnam until 2005, and then only for three days. People told her that she would feel at home there, but the sense of connection never came. She plans to return in a couple of years, with her two sons. She jokes that the boys feel more Vietnamese than she does. They have learned this from their Australian father, who has been to Vietnam many times on business, speaks fluent Vietnamese, and is fascinated by Vietnamese culture. He is, says Jen, the opposite to her—he is Vietnamese on the inside, and white on the outside.

The stories of the other intercountry adoptees are all shaped by the obvious fact that they are Asian on the outside; they share a visible difference from their parents and the wider Australian community. Their adoption was never a secret, and they have not suffered the shock of discovering it as adults. But the visible fact of their adoption has brought other problems. Like Jen they have had to cope with expectations, questions and sometimes abuse from strangers. Arriving as they did before the great influx of Asian migrants in the 1980s, these children were always marked as different by their school mates, however much they felt they were the same. Catherine was adopted in Malaysia by an Australian air force family. She went to school in a working-class suburb where life in the schoolyard was 'tough, really tough', though it did help to have two big all-Australian brothers. Like Jen, her parents told her to tough it out: 'Sticks and stones will break your bones but names will never hurt you'. 'Don't worry, you're part of the family. You're Australian'.

Simon Keogh, adopted from Vietnam before the babylift, is unusual amongst the Asian adoptees in our study in admitting to any problems of adjustment. He says that he had 'no issues' with his adoption until he hit puberty, when what he describes as the usual 'teenage identity crisis' was exacerbated in his case by being Asian in a white country. He believes that the anger and emotional turmoil he suffered are quite common amongst intercountry adoptees.

Simon speaks of his teenage crisis calmly, without any suggestion of ongoing trauma. All the Asian adoptees present as admirably mature people, very self-aware and secure in their responses. But one issue carries an emotional load for most of them. In the same way that the Australian adoptees have struggled with the search for their origins, the intercountry group have had to deal with the emotions raised by the prospect and the reality of a return to the land of their birth.

For some, this emotion is present in their reluctance to return. Some understand the return as an obligation, put upon them by parents and friends. Jen went very reluctantly. She deliberately limited her visit to Vietnam to three days on the way to a longer holiday in Thailand. 'I didn't want to stay too long', she says; 'I didn't want it to be too intense'. Others have set out on a long search for their origins, armed with stories about their adoption and copies of birth papers which have generally proved to be false. Sue Bylund has searched for nine years for the truth about her origins. She has visited Vietnam five times, scouring the country for clues. Now she has little faith in what people tell her; only DNA testing will convince her. But she is still searching.

For most of the Asian adoptees the return to country does not involve the search which obsesses so many of those adopted in Australia: the search for the mother who gave birth to them. This is probably due to the sheer impossibility of making this connection in a war-torn country like Vietnam. Catherine, the woman adopted by an Australian air force family, might have had a better chance of finding her mother in Malaysia. Her adoptive parents had known her mother before Catherine was born, so she has her name and address and details from the birth hospital. But all proved to be dead-ends.

The only adoptee on the website who has made contact with her birth mother was born in Nepal. She contributed her story anonymously. It is the most frankly emotional of the Asian stories. This story teller was even more reluctant than Jen to make contact with her past. Her adopting mother began searching for her birth mother from the moment of her adoption, writing every year to the Nepalese orphanage asking for news. After twelve years the news came that her mother Laksmi had also been searching, and contact was made. Members of her adopted family made repeated visits to Nepal, but the young storyteller refused to join them. She found the idea of having another family out there 'pretty bloody freaky!' She 'constantly wondered about her birth mother', but kept putting off the reunion. In the end her decision to go was shaped by a sense of obligation to other adoptees—'knowing so many had searched in vain'—and by an almost unspoken fear that her mother 'could possibly die'.

She made the journey on her own, feeling that her Nepalese mother would prefer this; her adopting mother promised that if the need arose that she was only a plane-trip away. The two-week visit was a wild 'roller-coaster of emotions': 'incredible, exciting, distressing, frustrating, a ridiculously incredibly hard thing to do'. Aspects of Nepalese culture appalled her, especially its treatment of women; some members of her birth family made her boil with suppressed anger; all 300 of her relatives 'felt like they knew me, and I felt like they were complete strangers'. She only survived by telling herself not to react: 'just be here'; 'deal with it later'; 'debrief when you get home'. But in the end she found she had discovered a new place for herself. Like the Australian adoptee Christine Kowal whose birth records gave her an identity that didn't depend upon the affirmation of either of her two families, the storyteller from Nepal found a space between her family of birth and her family of adoption where she could make of herself what she wished.

There can be strength in finding this space between families, between cultures. Indigo Willing is an Australian academic working in the area of transnational studies and migration; she is also an adoptee from Vietnam whose story is included on the History of Adoption website. Indigo identifies in herself and the other Asian adoptees the same conflicted sense of identity which Jen Fitzpatrick described as Asian on the outside, white on the inside. And just as Jen first found a positive self-understanding amongst the Asian students she met at university, Indigo finds some resolution in her work with the organisation Adopted Vietnamese International. AVI brings together Vietnamese adoptees from all over the world, mostly via the internet. Members who feel a lack of identity in both their home cultures and in Vietnamese culture find in AVI a shared identity, a sense of authenticity, in the company of Vietnamese adoptees like themselves. In an increasingly multi-cultural and transnational world, their ability to find viable spaces 'in-between' cultures is perhaps the way of the future.

CONCLUSIONS

Most of the storytellers make some judgement about the success or otherwise of their adoption. Barry Ford had no doubts about it.

My adopted parents did at all times what they considered to be the best for me... All in all, very little to complain about.

Barry loved and respected his family, even though he felt he did not belong there. Most of the storytellers shared Barry's sense of affection and obligation. Many delayed their search for their other family, out of respect for the feelings of their parents. Some like Christine Kowal found their birth families, and then worked hard to repair a relationship with parents who did not cope well with that discovery.

Storytellers whose memories are painful can still feel positive towards the parents who adopted them. An anonymous writer who is reduced to tears by 'grief and depression' by her memories writes that 'There are good aspects to adoption. I love my family, even if I cannot be open with them'. Only a few of the contributors report actively bad parenting, like the man who told his mother that 'I don't believe I had a good childhood, I was abused both physically and emotionally'. But even those who did have a good childhood suffer from that sense of not belonging.

Von Coates is an adoptee and also a trained social worker who has worked in adoption counselling. She makes a bitter comment on the question of success.

> I had what is usually described as a successful adoption and was a 'happy adoptee'—that is I didn't act out, cause trouble or appear to be in pain.

But her pain was real.

> I have engaged in therapy, counselling a number of times and have had to work very hard to come to terms with my trauma. It has taken me many decades to reach a point of acceptance regarding my adoption.

Von's pain is widely shared. David Hyland writes to the website specifically because

> I wanted to record my story in some way and also to express a positive story in amongst some truly saddening tales. I am passionate about adoptees and their experiences and I want to get across that there are definitely positive outcomes. I know through reading and group discussions that these can be rare... I know that this is tough a lot of the time, but we are special tough people and we must remain so through trying times.

The last word in this chapter goes to a contributor who does not tell a story, but simply writes about being adopted. For her, finding 'the space between' is both pain and comfort.

> The adopted child is unique, there is no one else like you in your family, this can be a gift and a burden.

> This singularity in the world is difficult, you are alone on this journey, until one day, you see someone who is the same shape as you, the way they smile, move their hands when they speak, stare out of a photograph, ah, you didn't invent yourself totally, these things that you are have come from somewhere, handed down to you, flesh and blood, belonging.

> But even then, sometimes it is too late, the 'return home' has come after too many years away. And although there is a relief in finding people who are like you, you don't really fit in there either, a visitor in your own family tree.

> The adopted limbo of longing and imperfect attachment becomes your own private comfort, somewhere between family and friend, somewhere between two lives, somewhere between flesh and blood, somewhere between loyalty and obligation.

> It is a strange and precarious place you find yourself in.

CHAPTER 2

THE PAIN OF MOTHERING

I am a Natural Mother who was the victim, as was my first born, to an illegal and forced adoption in 1973. This happened to many Mothers thousands in fact here in Australia I assure you from about 1940 to early 1980. I will not refer nor allow others to refer to me as either a birth Mother or a relinquishing mother. Both titles are degrading and inaccurate. As to what really happened. I am not a mere incubator as a birth mother suggests just of use until you have given birth then brutally discarded, nor am I a relinquishing mother. I never gave my permission for my precious first born, baby, a daughter to be snatched so barbarically from me the minute she was born on my 17th birthday 11-9-1973 and put up for adoption. Nor did I ask to be heavily sedated and given anti lactation medication. Nor have I ever found any Mother who willingly gave up a baby or child for adoption and doubt I ever will. I always wanted and loved my baby but was denied my Motherhood by others who should have known better.

Judith Hendriksen is a mother separated from her child by adoption. These are the opening words of her story as she posted it on the History of Adoption website.[2]

This chapter looks at mothers and their experience of adoption. It includes both mothers separated from their children by adoption, and adopting mothers. It draws on the stories that mothers have told, to researchers and to public inquiries. There is not much joy in these stories, and where it exists it is mostly mixed with pain.

---

2   Stories in Chapter 2 are drawn from the Monash History of Adoption website
     http://artsonline.monash.edu.au/historyofadoption/ and from submissions made to the
     Senate Community Affairs References Committee inquiry into the *Commonwealth
     Contribution to former forced adoption policies and practices*, February 2012 http://
     www.aph.gov.au/Parliamentary_Business/Committees/Senate_Committees?url=clac_
     ctte/completed_inquiries/2010-13/comm_contrib_former_forced_adoption/index.htm

It has been said that adoption is inevitably about loss: loss of identity for adopted children, as we saw in our last chapter; loss of motherhood for mothers separated by adoption, as we shall see here. And adopting mothers who are infertile also struggle with loss: loss of the child that could have been born to them. A psychologist told a conference on adoption in 1982 that the psychic burden of childlessness affects both those who have born children and lost them—to adoption, and in other ways—and those unable to bear children.[3]

We return to the pain of adopting parents towards the end of this chapter. First we deal with the much more pressing—and public—pain of mothers separated from their children by adoption.

SEPARATED BY ADOPTION

There are about a score of stories from mothers like Judith on the History of Adoption website. These are only a small sample of those that can be read online on Australian sites. Over the last decade mothers have contributed their stories to a series of government inquiries, most recently to the Senate Inquiry into the Commonwealth Contribution to Former Forced Adoption Policies and Practices. Hundreds of the submissions made to this inquiry come from mothers separated by adoption, and our account here draws on these stories as well as those posted on our website. Like Judith, most of these mothers are writing from pain and anger at wrongs done to them decades ago, and often only recently admitted to memory.

The pain in these stories means they are not easy to read. Most follow a similar plot. A number of voices from our website have been brought together to tell this heart-breaking story.

An unmarried underage girl discovers she is pregnant: 'I was terrified, frightened and alone. I couldn't tell anyone due to the shame'. She is sent by family or takes herself to a home for unmarried mothers: 'My father is disgusted with me and soon I am on my way to Newcastle and a government-run home for unmarried mothers'. She finds then or earlier that she is expected to give up her baby for adoption: 'We were actively discouraged from talking about our babies; there was a strict adoption-only policy'. She doesn't accept this: 'Feeling my baby move inside me made my pregnancy real for me and I planned a life with my baby'. But she

---

3   For the psychologist's paper see Judith Briley, 'Childlessness'. In *Changing Families: Proceedings of the Third Australian Conference on Adoption*, edited by R. Oxenberry. Adelaide, 1982: 354–358.

finds no alternatives: 'I kept hoping that some miracle would happen and I would be able to keep my baby, but no such miracle took place'.

In hospital she suffers lengthy, painful and generally unsupported labour: 'During my 21 hour labour I was left totally alone and was in so much pain that I wanted to die'. She is usually blocked from seeing her baby at birth: 'at the moment of birth, the midwife held a pillow in front of my face so I wouldn't see the baby I had carried for nine months'. After birth her requests to see and hold her child are usually ignored: 'Like so many other Mothers I did not see my baby. I did not hold her kiss her or even smell her'. Her claims to keep her baby are brushed aside: 'I was told I was selfish to want to keep my child, if I loved him I would want him to have 2 parents and a better life than I could give him'.

Usually she comes to believe she has no option but to give up her child: 'the JP pushed the papers toward me and through my tears I signed'.

Returning to the family that rejected her pregnancy, she is told 'to forget about it, to get on with her life'. She grieves for the lost child, usually in silence and continuing shame, for twenty or thirty years, and then begins actively searching for her, or is found by her. For these story-tellers the reunion is rarely the beginning of a satisfying relationship. Most report on-going pain: 'I can remember every moment of my time in that hospital and every waking moment the events are in my head and affect my everyday life'.

All of these stories come from the peak period of Australian adoption, the 1960s and early 1970s. Other stories could be told from this period. We know from the statistics that many single mothers—perhaps a third of them—kept their babies. We know too that thousands of women separated by adoption in these years have chosen not to speak out about their experiences. We can only guess the reasons for their silence, but some believed and continue to believe that their decision to adopt was the right one; we will meet one such woman later in the chapter. But for all that, the women who are speaking out tell a story which captures the lived experience of most single mothers in this period—whatever sense they made of it then or make of it now. In particular, it captures the process by which these women's children became potential products in the baby market.

PREGNANT

There is no single story about how these women became pregnant. Some were sexually inexperienced and still living at home; Judith did not understand what was happening to her when she was 'interfered with' by a friend of her elder brother's. Marilyn Murphy told the Senate inquiry:

> I was 18 when I met my first boyfriend, and as was quite common in those days (I had been raised in a strict religious atmosphere) I knew very little about sex. My first sexual experience could only be described as date rape.

Others were living independently. Jill Roz tells how in the year 1968:

> I am away from my childhood home, doing my nursing training and enjoying freedom from parental control. This includes lots of drinking and partying, where I meet an older Canadian man (I am 19) and become pregnant.

When Jill wrote to her lover

> my letter to Canada comes back 'address unknown' though the envelope has been opened.

Other women were in a 'stable relationship' or even living with the fathers of their children. Some like Margaret Nonas found that their partners 'did not wish to get married and take responsibility for a child', but in several cases the fathers wished to claim their children and marry their partners. Sometimes one or both sets of parents intervened. Barbara Maison told an inquiry that

> Our parents would not let us marry. We were not involved in any discussion, except that we could not keep our baby as neither of our families would, nor could afford to assist us to keep our child until we managed to get on our feet.

Couples who persisted in wishing to marry were vigorously discouraged by the threat that, in Elizabeth Edwards' words, 'my fiancé William Edwards would go to jail for carnal knowledge'. Barbara Maison reports that she and other pregnant girls lived in fear of visits from social workers from the Child Welfare Department.

> The threat of the 'Welfare' was enough to make your blood run cold, as if you had 'done it' too many times you would go into the 'Home of Good Shepherd'… until you were eighteen [and]… the boyfriend would be charged with 'Unlawful Carnal Knowledge' and would have to go to Court and possibly gaol.

It was common practice for pregnant young women to be sent away to 'unmarried mothers homes' for the later part of their pregnancy. Country girls were sent to the city; city girls were sent interstate: from Adelaide to

Melbourne, and occasionally Perth; from Tasmania to Melbourne; from Brisbane to Sydney. Marilyn Murphy wrote that

> My mother became hysterical, when she realised I was pregnant, she was bereft about the neighbours, the relatives, and the church members finding out her daughter was pregnant Out-of-Wedlock… It was decided that I go to a home for unmarried mothers… so that I would not be seen by others who would make judgment, on my parents and myself… My parents felt they had failed miserably.

When Judith Hendriksen's pregnancy was discovered:

> My parents blindly followed the advice from our local GP in a small country town… He said that adoption is the only option as a single teenager and he also highly praised St Anne's unmarried mothers home in Perth. My parents sent me there when I was about 4 or 5 months pregnant, so they wouldn't have to face the shame I had supposedly put on them, by getting myself pregnant.

Robyn Cohen was unusual amongst these women. Although she felt that 'I was disgraced, and I had disgraced my family', her family did not send her away.

> I was living in a flat in my home town and at five months pregnant I finally plucked up the courage to tell my mother and ask if I could move back home. To her credit she welcomed me back but great shame was felt.

Robyn kept working until the baby was due.

> As I was still in my home town there was no point in pretending by wearing a wedding ring so I was a very visible 'unmarried mother'. Everywhere I went I felt and heard the animosity toward me. Society could not see past 'unmarried mother' to see the pleasant, quiet girl that I was.

Robyn understands now, as she tells her story, that it was that 'unmarried mother' tag that robbed her of her baby: she and thousands of others 'were deemed by society to be unfit mothers and therefore lost their children to adoption'. They also functioned, in Kate Inglis's term, as 'living mistakes'— examples to other young women of the fate that awaited girls who mis-behaved.

Jill Roz remembers being sent to 'a government-run home' in Newcastle. This was unusual; the 'unmarried mothers homes' were generally run by the churches: Anglican, Methodist, Presbyterian, Salvation Army, and Catholic. Parents who could afford it were charged fees to cover their daughters' expenses. Young women without this parental support usually had to work for their keep, sometimes in hospitals and orphanages attached to the homes. Evelyn Mundy told the Senate inquiry that

> When I was at Elim [a maternity home in Hobart] I worked and never saw any money. They reckoned there was a wage. I do not think anyone saw it. I cleaned floors, I was working in the laundry and I was also working in the labour ward, cleaning up after the mothers had their babies.

And where a 'babies home' operated alongside the 'mothers home' the girls' labour produced another source of income. New parents were charged healthy fees to cover the cost of the babies they were adopting.

In most of these homes—and certainly in those which took in girls without charging them fees—it was assumed from the outset that adoption was the only possible outcome for their babies. Barbara Maison remembers that

> The Matron was a formidable, cold person who ran the home very strictly for the pregnant girls. It was a given that you had to give up your child for adoption to stay in the home. She made it clear that my baby was not MY BABY—there was no way I was going to keep 'it' if I wanted to stay in the home. I had nowhere else to go.

Marilyn Murphy's memories of 'the home' are full of anger.

> I was ushered to my dormitory, I sat on the bed, looked out the window that had cement brick guards bordering it, and then I saw the high fence with barbed wire encircling the entire back area... I WENT INTO SHOCK. I WAS INCARCERATED, I WAS IN GAOL... When I inquired why there was such a high fence and the barbed wire, I was told that was to keep others out and keep us safe!!!! WHAT A LIE, IT WAS TO KEEP US LOCKED UP TO ENSURE THEY HAD OUR BABIES RIGHT FROM BIRTH. THEY ALREADY HAD DESPERATE COUPLES WAITING FOR MY DAUGHTER.

Some women tried to argue, without success. Judith Hendriksen remembers that

> I did tell a nun about two weeks before my daughter's birth that I don't want my baby adopted out. I was told it is not your baby and how could you be so selfish to even ask there are many deserving married infertile Christian couples who have everything a baby could want [when] you have nothing.

In 2010 the Perth Sisters of Mercy wrote to Judith, regretting their part in her separation from her daughter and 'deeply and sincerely' apologising for the trauma it caused. More recently a number of church groups have responded to the Senate inquiry by offering similar apologies to the women who passed through their institutions.

GIVING BIRTH

Giving birth was not a pleasant experience for anyone in the 1960s. Doctors and administrators tended to understand birth as a crisis requiring medical intervention, with little sense of the 'patient' as actively involved in the event. So women were uniformly immobilised, with their legs pulled up into stirrups and their pains and senses dulled by far heavier doses of drugs than those used today. But single mothers suffered other indignities.

Margaret Nonas came back to Australia to have her baby after the man she was living with refused to take responsibility for the child. After their initial shock her parents 'took it in their stride and looked after me financially and emotionally before and after the birth of my son'. She saw her own doctor in the months before the birth; he mentioned adoption but she told him that she wanted to keep her child, and that her parents supported her decision.

Margaret's story is precise in its detail, reflecting careful research and documentation.

> I was admitted to the Western Suburbs Hospital, Newcastle, on the night of May 31st, 1967 at approximately 11.30pm. My paperwork states that I was a Mrs. and not a Miss, which I believe my Doctor did to protect me from adoption. I arrived with baby clothes and though frightened was looking forward to having my child.

Margaret made the mistake of telling an apparently sympathetic nurse that she was unmarried, and from that moment on her attitude changed and she treated me as if I was less than human. I was alone in the Labour Ward and very frightened as most new mums are and as the pain worsened I became upset. I was told to shut up and put up with the pain as I had gotten myself into this situation.

As the night went on she was given some medication; her medical record shows that 'among the drugs were barbiturates and an anti-psychotic'.

At approximately 6.30am I was in a great deal of pain and asked the same nurse how much longer I had to go, she had just examined me so would have been aware of my progress. Her answer was that I had all day to go yet and just to shut up and get on with it.

The website of the Senate inquiry carries a number of stories similar to Margaret's. Linda Eve wrote:

I was treated inhumanely. A nurse even told me the pain I was experiencing was punishment for getting pregnant before marriage. I was ignored and left alone with the contractions until the birthing began. I had no idea what to expect. They shouted at me, and then pushed a gas mask onto my face. They made comments about me, but didn't talk to me at all.

Worse was to come. Less than two hours after being told to shut up and get on with it Margaret gave birth

with the blankets piled over my face and a needle jabbed into my shoulder immediately upon giving birth. This needle contained Stilboestrel to dry up my breast milk. My baby was whisked away without me seeing him. I asked the nurse what sex the baby was and what the baby weighed, she told me that was not for me to know.

When Margaret's doctor arrived he insisted that she be given this information. But even he could not reverse the hospital's decision that as the child of an 'unmarried mother'—an unfit mother—the baby should and would be adopted.

Covering the mother's face with a pillow or a blanket and 'whisking away' babies intended for adoption was standard hospital practice in these years, in Australia and elsewhere. British nurses called it 'the rugger pass'. Hannah Spanswick writes that

I laboured on my own for twenty-seven hours and at the moment of birth, the midwife held a pillow in front of my face so I wouldn't see the baby I had carried for nine months.

Authorities believed that if the mother never saw the baby, she would not 'bond' with it. But all the mothers whose stories are online report ongoing grief at their loss. Hannah' story is typical:

> After the birth, I was transferred to the post-natal ward where I stayed for a day or so, among five other young mothers whose babies were brought out from the nursery every few hours to be fed. All I could do was turn my head away so I wouldn't see these young married women, feeding and cradling their babies.

Many like Margaret report being given anti-lactation drugs like Stilboestrel. The use of Stilboestrel was banned for pregnant women from the 1970s because of its potential dangers to people exposed to it in utero. Margaret's son died in 1995, only four years after their reunion, and she is 'still left to wonder if the drugs I was given during labour contributed to his death'.

Many report wandering the hospital wards trying to find the child they had lost. Kathy Maczkowiack remembers that

> I was taken to a ward with other mothers, mothers who had their babies brought to them. I asked to see my baby but this was refused, I left my bed continually and went looking for her but was taken back to my room. This was very distressing for me.

Judith Hendriksen writes that

> The most vivid memory I have after birth was when I was leaking milk from my breasts in the bathroom. In my head I recall thinking I would like to feed my baby natural Mothers milk. I was refused access to my own baby, and instead was told to stay put and given tablets quite a few I was told these were to dry my milk up, then the nun put a binder tightly around my breasts even that one act was abusive brutal and barbaric to say the least.

Dot Buckland was isolated with other single mothers on a hospital veranda, but

> you could hear the babies in the main ward with their mothers, we never saw our babies... you didn't mix with the other mothers, and

you didn't have much nursing interaction either, so it was almost like a baby factory, when I think back.

MOTHERHOOD DENIED

Margaret Nonas came into hospital with baby clothes, expecting to take her baby home. But it was not to be.

> On the fourth morning I said to my Doctor that I wanted to keep my baby, he left the room and returned with the Matron, the Head Sister and another woman, who carried paperwork. I was told I was selfish to want to keep my child, if I loved him I would want him to have 2 parents and a better life than I could give him. With four powerful people surrounding me and in my very distressed, drugged, emotional state, I agreed to give my child his 'better life'...

> I was sent home that day, together with my baby clothes and told to forget about him and get on with my life and get married some day and have more children and be happy for the gift I had given some childless couple.

Nearly all the mothers whose stories are online did not want to give up their babies. But once they were on the production line it was hard to get off. The two big women's hospitals in Melbourne and Sydney, the Royal Women's Hospital and Crown Street Hospital, handled between them more than half of all the thousands of adoptions that took place every year in the 1960s. It was established practice at both hospitals to mark the files of single mothers with initials indicating that their babies were for adoption: 'BFA' in New South Wales, Baby For Adoption, and 'A' in Victoria—'A' for Almoner, or social worker, which meant the same thing, given that only single mothers were referred to the hospital's social work department. This happened whether or not the mother had indicated an interest in adoption. Linda Eve told the Senate inquiry that

> My medical records have 'BFA' stamped on them... even though I said from the start I wanted to keep my baby. So it's clear to me they had the adoption of my child as their intention all along.

Once the file was marked, single mothers generally received the same treatment: instant removal of babies, anti-lactation drugs, and in the days immediately after the birth, frequent visits from social workers insisting that if they loved their babies they would give them up.

State laws differed in their detail, but across the 1950s and 1960s mothers could not legally give consent until at least five days after birth, and that consent could usually be revoked before the adoption order was made. Single mothers were told none of this. Nor were they told about the small amounts of government aid sometimes available to them in the form of sickness and unemployment benefits. Margaret Nonas writes that

> At no time was I told that there was financial assistance to keep my child, or told that there was a time period in which I could still get my baby back. I was told never to look for him, as he would be sent interstate. I eventually found out that he was only 12 miles from me the whole time I lived in Newcastle.

Many mothers report physical and mental duress to make them sign the necessary consent form. Others remember being tricked into signing, or never signing at all. Others were told lies: that their babies had already been adopted and could not be reclaimed, or even that their babies had died.

Most of these women returned to their parents' homes; they had nowhere else to go. Mothers and fathers who had refused to support them now refused to talk about it; they were to 'shut up and get on with their lives'. Alison Wright writes that the birth of her child was induced 'due to the fact that my parents wanted me home for Christmas so my absence didn't have to be explained'. Jill Roz's father

> sent me a letter telling me we would all just pretend it never happened and get on with my life, and they had arranged a late admission to university for me. Everything seemed surreal, like it was happening to someone else.

Judith Hendriksen was deeply depressed.

> When I returned home to country town after my baby was stolen from me I went off the deep end so to speak? I still hid myself in my parents house for a time, not sure how long exactly as even though not pregnant then must have still felt the shame. I did however venture outdoors at night and can recall walking in my pyjamas late at night searching for my baby everywhere in the streets and gardens. I guess my brain couldn't accept that my baby was truly gone. My parents didn't know what to do with me.

SEARCHING

Judith's grief was open and raw. Other women hid their feelings and never spoke of their experience. But they too were remembering and searching: buying a card for their child's birthday, looking into the faces of passing children of about the right age. One woman knitted twelve jumpers in ascending sizes, one a year for each year of her child's life. Others later joined activist groups and worked towards changing the adoption laws to allow people involved in adoption to access their records.

Many women continued to feel shamed by their experience. They felt ashamed at being the mother of an illegitimate child. They felt ashamed of having given up that child, in order, as they were told, to be a good mother. Many were numbed by their shame and grief. Jill Roz reports that seven years after she lost her son:

> One morning there was something about adoption on the radio, and I started to cry. Once I started for that first time, I could not stop. A friend came in during this avalanche of tears and I told her about the adoption. To my surprise she didn't look at me with disgust but compassion and love.

Adoption records were opened in all states except Queensland by the mid-nineties, and mothers and adopted children could begin reaching out to each other. The search was often hesitant, and the outcome difficult. Alison Wright waited for years before beginning.

> It wasn't until 1996… that I began the search. As luck would have it, my son, James, is a computer freak, and so it took a quick search on Google to find him. I wrote an outreach letter to him and had a positive reply back within two days. I arranged to fly to Adelaide for the weekend to meet him for the first time.

The reunion was not a great success:

> I was absolutely terrified at the prospect of having to explain to him why I had given him away. At our first meeting he reached out to me to give me a hug—I couldn't respond and so I inadvertently pushed him away. We spent the weekend together but the strain this put on both of us was huge and it was a relief for us both to say goodbye at the airport. On arriving back in Melbourne I couldn't stop crying. I

cried for 5 days. All that grief that I had never allowed myself to feel came out and I didn't have the strength to stop it.

Jill Roz's reunion with her son was something of a disaster. She began looking in 1992; to her surprise 'Jigsaw found him without trouble', and a meeting was arranged.

> On the way into the city that day, I cried uncontrollably on the train; I just could not believe this long-awaited day had arrived. For years I had celebrated his birthday by feeling miserable and getting drunk, and wondering what had happened to him…
>
> At 11 am outside MacDonald's I saw him, stood up and we shook hands. I couldn't take my eyes off him; we went to have a coffee and the waitress commented that we must be mother and son, we looked so much alike. He asked me about the medical history of my family. Then we got on a ferry to Manly. He told me how he looked more like his mother's side of the family. I couldn't believe what I was hearing. Wasn't I his biological mother? I guess he was letting me know he was sticking with his adoptive parents.

Her son had allocated 3 hours to their meeting. They went over to Manly and back again on the ferry, and that was it. Jill felt 'horribly upset'.

> The reunion was so distressing, it actually was worse than the adoption experience. When I got back home I went into hiding for a week or so, I didn't want to have to tell people how awful it had been, when I had had such high expectations. I haven't seen him again.

Many of the online stories tell a similar tale of high expectations followed by disappointment. As we saw in chapter 1, the search for the lost mother rouses contradictory feelings in adopted people: at once desire for reunion and fear of rejection. Mothers also suffer these contradictions. Alison felt that she had inadvertently rejected her son when she could not embrace him, and he responded by withdrawing.

> James and I corresponded by email but after a few months I realised that he didn't want contact. He stated that he had agreed to meet with me purely to satisfy his curiosity and having done that, he wanted nothing more from me.

But the story has a happy ending—at least at the time of writing. Alison accepted her son James' decision, but 'let him know if he changed his mind, I would welcome him'. Thirteen years later contact was renewed, via the web. Alison writes that

> Needless to say, I was extremely wary as I knew I couldn't go through the heartbreak again. To cut a long story short, James and I are now slowly building trust between one another.

Her conclusion is entirely positive—a rare thing amongst these stories of continuing loss.

> Reunion with my son put the smile back on my dial and I now feel content. All the loose family ends have been tied together and while we all have our own lives and are separated by distance, we are connected for life. It's been a long, hard road with many lessons to be learned along the way but the end result has led to feelings of inner peace—feelings I treasure and will hold on to for as long as possible.

AN ALTERNATIVE VIEW

Christine approached the History of Adoption team because she wanted to tell us a different story from those she found on our website and saw on television. She didn't want to deny the truth of other people's experience, but wanted her voice to be recognised. Christine is not her real name; she chose to use this pseudonym.

Christine's account follows the same storyline as others told in this chapter, but the meaning she gives it is different. She fell pregnant in 1971. She was eighteen years old, a year out of school. 'I was a bit ratty in those days'. The father was someone she had gone to school with. She didn't tell him, and thinks in retrospect that was a mistake, but 'we were both so young'. Rather she took control of the situation in the only way that she could.

> When I found I was pregnant I thought oh God I have to do something about this… I knew someone who had been in a similar circumstance so I organised—I spoke to her about where she had gone and I organised the whole thing, I contacted the nuns and I organised to go there… I had to have a plan for this before I told my parents and I did.

Christine always intended that her baby should be adopted. Her parents accepted her plan, though her mother suggested that she should go to the home for single mothers 'a bit earlier', 'she was concerned about people knowing I was pregnant'.

There have recently been criticisms in the press about the treatment of single mothers in this home, but Christine insists that her experience was positive. This may have been because 'I had my driver's licence which not everybody did—I drove the nuns around—I got out a bit more than the others'. She was used to living with nuns; she had gone to a Catholic boarding school. 'And anyway I was there for my pregnancy'. When her son was born she was given him to hold, 'which was nice'. She was told that she could see him in the nursery, but she chose not to do this; 'it was too hard'. After the mandatory four days 'the adoption papers came and I signed'. Then she 'cried for quite some time'. The social worker at the hospital came and told her that she had found a suitable family to adopt the child, matching Christine's in class and circumstances.

At the time Christine assumed the adoption would happen immediately. Later she discovered that her son had stayed in the hospital for about five weeks. She felt guilty about this, but heard from a nurse who had worked in the nursery that 'they used to pick up the adopted babies'. After that 'I didn't feel so bad'.

Christine never thought that her son would come looking for her; 'I thought he won't do that', only girls are interested in that kind of thing. But he did. They wrote to each other for some time, developing a relationship. 'Then we met, and that was lovely'. 'Then I met his parents who were just fabulous, and that was such a relief to me'. Now they see each other about once a year. Christine believes the reunion has been a success because 'neither of us had any expectations that it would be a mother and son relationship'. She does not claim motherhood of her son: 'His mother is his mother'.

MOTHERHOOD CREATED

An adoption conference in 1982 heard the story of a husband and wife from Greece 'with nine years of infertility and a desperate longing for children'.[4] They had come to the point of considering adoption when the wife was diagnosed with cancer of the ovaries, requiring a hysterectomy. She was

---

4   For this story and the comments below on childlessness see Jan Aitken, 'Who Are the Childless?' In Oxenberry, (ed.), *Changing Families*, 349–353. The social worker's comment is from p.352.

devastated by the threat to her life, and even more by the loss of her womb. Added to all this, given her poor prognosis and his age, they could no longer hope to be accepted as adopting parents. The social worker in charge of their case reported that

> Their grief and confusion is overwhelming. I feel so awful not being able to promise her a child. She might have only three years to live and spend all of it grieving.

The urge to become a mother (and a father) runs deep within our lives. Social attitudes validate this urge. This is perhaps less true today, but last century childless married couples were made to feel ashamed. 'People make you feel second-rate. They make you feel that you've done something awful because you don't have kids'. To admit to being unable to have children drew comments like 'not doing it right hey?' Or 'Need a hand mate, wink, wink, nudge, nudge'. A wife observed that

> I noticed if I was at a children's party, I was on the outer, left out, but I just kept this sadness to myself and put on this big smiling face.

Adoption was generally understood as a cure for infertility: a way that men could become more 'mature, responsible, reliable and virile'; and women more 'warm, feminine, credible and productive'. And people who chose to adopt were recognised as generous and open-hearted.

Today the voices of mothers separated by adoption dominate public debate. Adopting parents have found themselves characterised as selfish and unfeeling. Very few have chosen to make their stories public. Like Christine, Merle chose to give us her story because she has a different truth to tell. She does not speak for anyone else; her training as a psychologist colours her experience in particular ways. Again, this is not her real name.[5]

Merle has adopted 3 children, the first in 1959. It was her infertility that led her to be interested in adoption. One baby miscarried, another died as a toddler, a third was aborted at eight months with massive abnormalities. Before conceiving the third child Merle and her husband explored the option of adoption with the social worker at the Royal Women's Hospital. Her husband was a doctor, and the couple met all the qualifications for adoptive parenthood. The social worker told Merle to go ahead with one

---

5   For a discussion of the characterisation of adopting parents, see Margaret Sandelowski, 'Fault Lines: Infertility and Imperilled Sisterhood'. *Feminist Studies* 16(1) (1990): 33–51.

more pregnancy, and if the baby was not healthy 'we can arrange to have an adoption'. So Merle went into the pregnancy knowing that one way or the other 'I would have a baby'.

After the loss of the third child Merle maintained her milk supply by expressing great quantities of breast-milk—'I was a good Jersey'. She was prepared to keep expressing for months, but 'a fortnight later there was a baby for me'. They brought her home rejoicing.

But, Merle told us, 'it was too soon'.

> I hadn't grieved long enough about the loss of my last baby. I used to have floods of tears going down over my breasts when I was feeding her—how could you have not been mine—real poignant sadness just kept sweeping over me as I fed this beautiful, beautiful child.

And for 30 days the baby was doubly not hers. Legally the 'relinquishing mother' had 30 days in which she could revoke her consent.

> That was a terrible time—breastfeeding this baby who was increasingly mine, knowing that there was a likelihood that I would have to hand her back.

Looking back she realises that at the time 'I had no feelings of empathy with the relinquishing mother at all… It was like her versus me, and I wanted a baby'. In retrospect Merle feels she would have had more empathy with a woman driven to abduct a baby. And after all, she says, 'What's the difference?' Adoption is a form of abduction, a socially approved way 'to steal a baby from a caring woman'.

Merle's understanding of her own feelings is more sophisticated than most. But it seems that adopting mothers often share her conflicted feelings for the mothers of their children. A researcher in the 1990s drew emotional responses when she asked adopting women about the mothers they had supplanted. They expressed gratitude:

> We felt she had given us something we could never have had… we always prayed for her

but also guilt:

> I think about her more than I thought I would… It's almost like one day I'll have to answer to a higher authority.

and denial:

> I never thought of her again... This was my baby now. I'd do the best
> I could... Well, I did think of her once [said struggling with tears].[6]

For these women the Birth Mother was a continuing presence in their lives.

> I prayed for her... We were a party of three, a three party situation...
> the Birth Mother, the baby and me... every birthday I'd think of
> her... Every birthday I'd cry.

The institution of adoption which set up birth mothers and adopting
mothers as enemies also hid from them the truth: that their sufferings were
two sides of the same coin. The figure of the Good Mother—warm, generous,
fertile only within marriage—has brought pain to all women unable to reach
that ideal.

A HAPPY ENDING?

Emma Anderson posted the story of her daughter Grace's adoption on the
History of Adoption website to let 'everyone to know what we know and
have been given the opportunity to understand about international adoption'. She wanted to counter 'the misrepresentation that children are better
left in orphanages or on the street in their home countries'.

Emma and her husband decided to adopt in 2007.

> After having two biological sons and suffering from post natal
> depression after both of them, my husband and I decided we still
> wanted to have 3 or 4 children. We wanted more children and there
> were children out there that needed families so it seemed pretty
> simple. The altruistic view is—put them together.

Emma was not worried about loving an adopted child less than those she
had given birth to. Her post natal depression meant that

> We had no natural bonding moment at birth with our sons—the
> hormonal imbalance actually created an opposite effect.

Emma learned how to love her sons 'more and more each day', to accept them
as a gift. 'They were children we received and placed in our care by God'.

---

6   Susan Gair, 'The Impact of the Queensland Legislation on the Lives and Families of
Adoptive Mothers'. In *Has Adoption a Future? Proceedings of the Fifth Australian
Adoption Conference, Sydney, August 1994*, edited by Margaret McDonald. Sydney:
Post Adoption Resource Centre, 1994: 130–139, quotations are on p. 137.

The Andersons seriously considered the option of permanent foster care.

> In our eyes the latter was the same as adoption. The child is a ward of the state and we are their carer until the age of 18. We worked through our concerns about how contact with the birth mother and siblings may confuse the family balance and saw this as a real alternative.

Then an overseas posting to Hong Kong offered the option of adopting 'without the expense and long waiting lines back in Australia'. They were hopeful at first about adopting from China, but the waiting lines were long there too. They found contacts at an orphanage in Cambodia and a lawyer to work with—but then the Cambodian government shut down the application process 'because they had to appear to be doing something about child trafficking'. They decided on Ethiopia because they could work through an agent there and bypass the bureaucracy.

Emma hoped to adopt two girls, possibly sisters.

> When we considered that our daughter would be a different race as well as a different gender to the two boys, we decided that having a sister going through the same things would add a level of comfort and familiarity that I couldn't provide no matter how hard I tried.

But in the end she settled for one, Grace. Her story lingers on Grace's physical condition when she was 'rescued'.

> She was sitting on a mat picking up crumbs from the ground next to her... Grace had skin hanging off her bones, a bloated stomach and a blank stare. She had been found at a police station in Agaro (Jimma region) at 9 months, weighing only 3.5kg. By now at 11 months she weighed 6kg. They had fed her an egg every day, given her formula and some medicine with vitamins. Apparently they also wormed her, but judging by the 15cm worm that I pulled out of her mouth in December after a coughing fit—the worming was not effective. I agreed straight away to adopt her and picked her up for a cuddle.

There were still more bureaucratic mountains to climb, described in graphic detail for the benefit of others who might benefit from the Andersons' example. In the end they fly home with Grace, 'a tiny bundle with heavy breathing and big eyes'.

We had a baptism in our church back home with our family and friends and the minister I have known for over 15 years. It was a special day, full of tears of joy and relief.

When Emma posted her story, Grace was 20 months old.

She is happy, laughs a lot (especially with her brothers), is learning to speak, throws and kicks balls, puts dolls into little bags and carries them around the house and always tries to put shoes on so that we will take her on an outing. She says up peese (up please), ball, dog, dada, mumum, eyes, her brothers names, can roar like a lion, dances like an African tribal dancer... presses every button she can find, hones in on the kitchen if someone is cooking, claps hands, waves at people and even throws tantrums every now and again. Her photo is on every friend and family members' fridge, wall or mantle. She is prayed for daily and people wait for updates via Email, Photo bucket or Skype calls. None of us can get enough of this precious little girl Grace.

And yet, despite all this joy, Emma too is haunted by thoughts of her baby's mother. She worries about 'this complicated world, where some mothers have so much to raise their children with, and others have to give up due to sickness or famine'. She tries to imagine the mother's grief:

As a mother walks away with shoulders slumped, a dead stare at the ground and complete hopelessness—wondering what will happen to the child that came from her womb—I imagine there are no tears left by this point.

The international market in children has almost entirely replaced the domestic market as a source of supply of 'precious babies' for Australian parents. Certainly these babies bring joy to families in Australia. But the loss to women in Ethiopia and the other 'supply' countries—women who surely would have raised these children if they could—must be balanced against Australia's gain.

Part II

PROCESS

CHAPTER 3

MAKING ADOPTION SAFE
AND RESPECTABLE

In the late 1950s 'The Adoption of Children Acts' were described in the Victorian parliament as

> possibly the best pieces of legislation on the statute-book. It is a thrilling experience to see young children brought into Judges' chambers, dressed with loving care and the affectionate and anxious adopting parents in their 'Sunday' best giving assurances to the Judge as to the future care and maintenance of a child. When the ceremony is over, they depart with the child to take it into a home where it will be assured of love and affection.

Parliamentarians were delighted with adoption because it seemed to be a solution to the longstanding problem—and public expense—of the unsupported child. Some knew adoption as a solution to infertility amongst friends or family. They contrasted present-day adoption with an 'evil' past where children were openly traded with little concern for their welfare.[7]

There was no place here for the voices of the single mother mourning for her lost child, the midwife who witnessed that distress, or the adoptee who was unhappily placed. This chapter explores the history of adoption in order to understand how a practice that was producing pain alongside joy came to be so highly praised.

ADOPTION UNREGULATED

In a society without welfare, there is no safety net for the care of children when family support fails. In the nineteenth and the first half of the twentieth century, this left the child of an unsupported single mother doubly

---

7   Adoption of Children Acts, *Victorian Parliamentary Debates* (Hansard), Legislative Council 1955–6: 879.

vulnerable, stigmatised both as evidence of the moral weakness of its mother and as a potential drain on the taxpayer. From the late 1840s the mothers, fathers or guardians of such children offered them for adoption in the classified advertising columns of colonial newspapers. The advertisements used a language of kindness or benevolence, but this only thinly disguised a market exchange. Advertisers praised the child's health and gentility in the hope of finding someone to take it off their hands. About ten per cent of advertisers offered money or goods—called 'premiums'—in the hope of increasing their chances.[8]

An 1885 newspaper article from the Victorian river port of Echuca provides a glimpse of the looseness with which children changed hands. Four children of a marriage in disarray were found wandering and brought before the court. The magistrate assigned the youngest to the mother, but judged that the father was best positioned to support the others. Angry that his wife refused to live with him, the father left the court and promptly disposed of the other three children to 'charitable persons who were willing to adopt them'. Adoption here was a convenient solution in which the state saw no reason to interfere.[9]

More commonly it was younger children that were on offer. Single mothers without the assistance of family would struggle to support a baby. The costs both to income and to reputation were high. Partners or parents were often willing to fund an adoption, and the midwives who made their income from delivering the children of single mothers were more than willing to make the necessary arrangements, charging a fee at every step in the transaction. Such midwives became known in their immediate areas as people who could supply babies for adoption. Absolute secrecy prevailed and no records were kept. In some cases, mothers who adopted used the services of midwives to deceive even their husbands into assuming that the new baby was theirs.

The willingness of midwives to become involved in this trade is evidence that there was a demand for children to adopt, a demand that was also reflected in the advertisements. Some were clearly seeking children for the work they could do in homes or on farms. But the wording of most of the

---

8   This story is told in more detail in articles by Shurlee Swain. See, for example, Shurlee Swain, 'Market Forces: Defining the Adoptable Child'. *Social Policy and Society*, 11(3) (2012): 399–414; and Marian Quartly and Shurlee Swain, 'The Market in Children: Analysing the Language of Adoption in Australia'. *History Australia* 9(2) (2012): 69–89.

9   'Echuca'. *The Argus*, 11 November 1885, 8.

advertisements suggests an increasingly sentimental exchange, the notion that someone else's 'unwanted' child could fill a gap in a childless home. A growing proportion of these advertisers expected to be paid for taking on the child, peaking at over forty per cent in the first decade of the twentieth century. Commentators assumed that some of these advertisers were not genuine, but rather were 'baby farmers' seeking to profit from other people's distress.

The term baby farmer was coined in England in the second half of the nineteenth century. It was used to describe women who offered to adopt infants in exchange for a fixed payment and then hastened them towards an early death. Several notorious Australian trials led to a demonisation of the much wider group of women who were paid to nurse the children of working mothers. Editorials condemned the 'she-devils' or 'hags' who specialised in the 'merciless' trade of baby farming, a 'legal butchering' which threatened the colonies' claims to civilisation. They told sensational stories of fictitious names and false addresses, assignations on street corners or railway stations, with babies changing hands several times, leaving no discernible trace. Sydney's Kate de Lawarie was reported as regularly answering advertisements from women seeking to have their children adopted. De Lawarie offered to act as an intermediary. The prospective adoptive parent, she would claim, lived in rural Mudgee and the only recompense she sought was the train fare. But she never made the journey, abandoning the babies nearby once the money was in her hand.[10]

Campaigns demanded an end to such practices in the interests of saving infant life. As a result legislation was passed in most colonies requiring places where women gave birth to be registered, and nurses to be licensed. These laws banned the payment of premiums in relation to adoption, but offered no assistance to mothers to support their own children. Nor did they open any legitimate avenues through which childless couples could obtain children. Not surprisingly, the advertisements continued. The impact of the baby farming scandals seems to have discouraged 'sellers' from offering a premium with the child, but 'buyers' increasingly asked to be paid for their efforts.

By the final decades of the nineteenth century there was a second route through which couples could adopt a child. From the 1870s children in state

---

10   The Kate De Lawarie case received extensive coverage in the press but see, for example, 'Alleged abandonment of infants'. *Sydney Morning Herald*, 23 February 1889, 8; and 'Professional Abandonment of Children. A Heartless Woman'. *South Australian Advertiser*, 27 February 1889, 5.

care were increasingly 'boarded out' to foster parents who were paid to look after them. Some of these parents came to want a more permanent arrangement, trading the weekly payments for security of possession and freedom from inspection. Orphanages and infant asylums noted a similar demand. The applicant willing to take a child without payment came to be seen as superior to the foster mother whose parenting was tainted by financial reward. Legislators liked the idea of children at once being freed from the lovelessness of an institutional life and ceasing to be a charge against the state. Within ten years of the introduction of boarding-out in South Australia, authorities claimed that three-quarters of the children had been adopted by their foster parents. Politicians in the neighbouring colony of Victoria were so impressed that they ordered child welfare officials to dispense with the 'stringent and vexatious' foster care regulations when applicants were prepared to adopt. The 'unwelcome visits from inspectors', newspaper editorials commented, were 'perpetual reminders that the children they are rearing as their own are not their own'.[11]

Adoptive parents wanted the assurance that a child could not be re-claimed, something which neither the private operators nor the child welfare authorities could provide. This desire for certainty was recognised by both sides of the advertising market, with sellers offering full possession while buyers insisted that the child should be entirely given up. Even so continuing contact was not uncommon. When she had to go into service, George Bolton's mother allowed him to be adopted by a neighbouring family. She visited him regularly and threatened to disrupt the adoption when the family announced their intention of moving interstate. The judge who heard the case was sympathetic but was not convinced that the mother could support her child. He compromised by ordering the adoptive parents to lodge a bond agreeing to return George to Victoria should his mother's situation change. Such sympathy was relatively uncommon. In other cases parents who sought to reclaim a child were reprimanded for having parted with the child in the first place.[12]

It was just such 'interference' that parents looking to adopt were anxious to avoid. Private operators tried to reassure their customers by promising secrecy and a veneer of legality. In the early years of the twentieth century,

---

11   See 'News of the Day'. *Sydney Morning* Herald, 10 January 1882, 5; and 'Adoptions', in 'The Industrial Schools'. *Argus*, 23 September 1880, 7. The editorial cited is 'Infant Preservation'. *Advertiser* (Adelaide), 31 October 1913, 14.

12   George Bolton's case is reported in 'Custody of a Child'. *Argus*, 30 September 1908, 9.

midwives Hannah Hurrell and Clarice Donaldson owned several private hospitals in Melbourne's inner eastern suburbs, catering primarily to a middle class clientele. Women were confined under false names, and their infants were transferred to adoptive parents and registered in their names. The midwives insisted that discretion was at the centre of their practice, because the mothers wanted to be able to pass the children off as their own. Private operators engaged solicitors to draw up adoption agreements, but reputable lawyers felt obliged to inform their clients that such agreements had no basis in law. State children's departments used similar agreements to set out the responsibilities of adoptive parents, but they too were unable to offer complete security. There was no legal mechanism that could remove a child from its family of birth and reconstitute it as part of another.[13]

Child welfare officials advocated the introduction of formal adoption from the 1890s. To make the prospect attractive to legislators they argued that the introduction of legal adoption would reduce the number of children needing to be maintained in state care. But colonial parliaments were slow to respond; there were no British precedents for such a law. Only the Western Australian parliament was prepared to legislate for legal adoption, in 1896. When the issue was raised again in South Australia in 1917 the Attorney-General responded that 'very serious objections' had been raised to the prospect of 'depriving a natural mother of the control of her children' and refused to proceed.[14]

By the following decade those objections had been brushed aside. Australians became aware that other jurisdictions had legislated for adoption. Articles from America and England were reprinted in local newspapers, presenting adoption as a benevolent act, freed of its older negative associations. Newspapers carried sympathetic stories about Hollywood stars who chose adoption as a way of building their families. The message was reinforced in popular films and novels in which children found parents and lived happily ever after, their families of origin completely erased.

Adoption became law in all the eastern states during the 1920s. The child welfare professionals who helped draft these laws were cautious about letting the free market reign. Although they believed that children needed to be freed from the control of parents they saw as feckless or immoral, their long years of administering boarding-out programs had left them well aware of the mixed motives of people hoping to adopt. Authorities in South Australia

---

13   For Hurrell and Davidson see 'Traffic in Babies'. *Argus*, 11 October 1913, 18.
14   *Official Reports of the Parliamentary Debates. Session 1924*, vol. 1. Adelaide: Government Printer, 1924 (2 vols): 454.

remembered the scandal that had followed the State Children's Department approval of an offer from a Victorian man to pay £1000 to adopt a young state ward. Sylvia Thomas had been living with her foster mother since she was five months old. The Department was accused of trafficking in human flesh, planning to sell the child to the highest bidder. Parliament over-ruled the decision, but the incident had exposed the inequalities involved in any adoption exchange.[15]

Sylvia's potential adopter claimed to have been attracted by her uncanny resemblance to his dead mother. Authorities learnt over time to question such motives. Applicants for older children were often more interested in their potential as workers than as family members. Families with lots of young children were suspiciously anxious to adopt girls in their early teens. Some men sought children for sexual purposes. In New South Wales a man who called himself Sir William Newton repeatedly advertised to adopt young boys, promising to make them his heir, only to sexually assault them. John McBroom, a pioneer settler on New South Wales's Manning River, regularly sought to adopt girls, offering a good home and limited pay without specifying the services that were required. Child welfare authorities argued that adoption without regulation allowed such problems to flourish. They shared with prospective parents the demand for secrecy and certainty, but insisted that legislation should preserve their right to decide who should be permitted to adopt.[16]

The adoption laws of the 1920s were tentative attempts at social experiment. They accepted the principle that the legal status of the adopted child should be aligned with that of the natural born child, but preserved some differences in terms of rights to inherit. In all states but Queensland, only judges or magistrates could authorise adoption, but a broad range of professionals were eligible to arrange adoptions. The principle of secrecy was embedded in the legislation, but in practice identifying information about the family of origin continued to be available to the adopting parents— though the reverse was far less common. Over the following decades these Acts were frequently amended, resolving problems as they arose. Most of these amendments worked to strengthen the claims of those who adopted and to further diminish the rights of the birth family.

---

15   'A Ward of the State'. *Advertiser*, 4 December 1913, 15.
16   'A Supposed Millionaire. Some Serious Charges'. *Brisbane Courier*, 5 March 1903, 5;
     Sydney Morning Herald, 17 December 1907, 6 March 1909, 28 July 1911.

LEGAL ADOPTION

Legal adoption offered a single solution to a multitude of social problems. 'The measure', one Victorian parliamentarian declared in 1928, 'will bring a lot of sunshine into many homes. It will give otherwise unfortunate children a better outlook, and take away the dread of many expectant mothers that their offspring may have to live in misery'. However, the legislation did not have the immediate impact which its advocates had expected. While families who had already adopted a child used the law to gain security of possession, new applicants did not rush the market, and the numbers of children in state care continued to grow. The practices of the past had cast a long shadow. If legal adoption was to succeed it had to be actively sold.[17]

While the law addressed the issue of security, it did nothing to dispel lingering doubts about the quality of the child available for adoption, the fear that as the child developed 'some unexpected and dreadful trait' might appear. Adoption advocates accepted the reality of this fear, retaining children until they were twelve to eighteen months old so that prospective adopters could be sure that they were developing normally. In some cases mothers remained in contact with their children during this phase, including breastfeeding them in the early weeks. Adoption agencies used every means available to display their proven 'products'. The Western Australian child welfare authorities boasted that they had 'all types of babies to choose from, passed as medically fit for adoption, and full family history given where possible'. Doctors and other experts, they added, 'confirmed... that these little mites, arriving out of the great unknown, are very apt to be unusually lovely, healthy and intelligent'.[18]

Melbourne's Mission of St James and St John paraded its babies at select meetings of supporters, and reported great success from its regular stall at the Melbourne Show where babies were on display. Other organisations ran paid advertisements at the movies, produced albums of photographs from which prospective parents could make their choice, and paraded the children at public events in order to maximise their popular appeal. Stories in the women's and children's pages of newspapers and magazines situated adoption as the solution to the problems of both childless women and abandoned children. Margaret, the problem page writer for the women's magazine, the

---

17 The parliamentarian's speech is reported in *Victorian Parliamentary Debates* (1928):1233.
18 See 'The Adopted Child'. Women's Column', by Villette'. *Mercury* (Hobart), 15 June 1929, 14; and 'Adopted Children. Girls in Great Demand'. *West Australian*, 7 September 1932, 12.

New Idea, invoked her experience of living next door to a babies' home to reassure her readers about the quality of the product on offer. The children that she saw out at play, she wrote, were 'not necessarily nitwits' but 'clean, healthy and quite quick on the uptake'. Their mothers were represented as of superior quality as well, 'beautifully dressed' women driving expensive cars, distressed at the prospect of parting with their child, but accepting that it was in the child's best interest. Even where children came from less affluent backgrounds, adoption before the age of five ensured that environment would overcome heredity.[19]

In a buyer's market prospective adopters set the terms. 'Frequently they specify the colour of the eyes and hair of the child they are looking for', Western Australian authorities noted, 'and we do our best to adhere to the specifications'. Prospective parents were advised to view the child to 'make sure that it appeals to them'. The preferences apparent in the classified advertisements proved hard to dislodge. New baby adoptions were comparatively rare, girls were preferred over boys, and blond, blue-eyed girls were the most popular of all. 'When little girls are available', one nurse commented, 'no-one will look at the boys'. Regular advertisements used by the Western Australian authorities to attract adoptive parents featured detailed descriptions of eye and hair colouring, ethnicity and respectability for each child.[20]

There was little place for birth parents in the post-legalisation market. The aim of legal adoption was to erase the child's origins. The role of the mother was restricted to delivering the child and then relinquishing it, grateful to be relieved of the stigma attached to single motherhood. Most mothers, a Melbourne babies' home matron insisted, were 'sensible' about the necessity for adoption, 'realising that it is best for their own future and their baby's if the child is taken into a home where it will find a father's as well as a mother's love'. Birth fathers were scarcely acknowledged at all. Parents who tried to make themselves visible were increasingly presented as threatening. Fears of blackmail or kidnap were used to justify the strengthening of secrecy provisions in the law. Parents were denied any knowledge of their child's new family, and any attempt to disrupt an adoption was made a criminal offence.

---

19   'Adopting a Child'. *New Idea*, 15 July 1938, 25; and 'Wants to Adopt a Child'. *New Idea*, 24 March 1939, 28.

20   'Adopted Children. Foster Parents Prefer Girls'. *West Australian*, 6 March 1933, 7; '"The Counsellor" Says There Is… Wisdom in Adopting Young Children'. *Courier-Mail* (Brisbane), 29 June 1940, 13; and '"There is a Shortage of Baby Girls Here". From Our Melbourne Correspondent'. *Advertiser*, 26 March 1936, 10.

While there was an understanding that a mother who could provide for her child might be anxious to reclaim it, there was universal agreement that relinquishment had to be permanent.[21]

In Melbourne, Oswald Barnett talked of adoption as part of a great national crusade to rescue the children of the slums and transform them into healthy, productive citizens. His 1948 pamphlet, *Is it safe to adopt a baby?*, summarising the outcomes for 100 of the first children adopted from the Methodist Babies' Home, served as powerful propaganda for the adoption cause. It showed conclusively that the adopted child who was taken in and loved was as well-adjusted in adulthood as any other. It was 'most encouraging', the medical director of the Children's Hospital wrote in his introduction, 'that children, whose original background was so sordid, should at this stage of their development be reported upon so favourably'.[22]

Even before Barnett demonstrated that adoption was safe, people were coming to believe that it was socially acceptable. In 1940 a lady volunteer in New South Wales reported that there were usually more suitable applicants than there were children available for adoption, an observation repeated in other states. The market reflected the same trend. In those states in which advertisements were still permitted, the number of people seeking to adopt exceeded those offering children for adoption for the first time in 1942, and the gap grew dramatically over the years that followed.[23]

Publicity around adoption moved from enticements to adopt to reports of growing waiting lists. Applicants felt frustrated in the face of an application process that they saw as unnecessarily bureaucratic. The preferences of the past were set aside as growing numbers of clamorous couples were willing to accept any baby that was on offer. 'The new baby could be a boy or girl, fat or thin, blond or brunette', declared a fictionalised mother, symbolically named Hope, 'just as long as it was theirs'. The comment comes from a humorous short story in the *Australian Women's Weekly* in which the social worker came unannounced while the applicants were hosting a large party. Not surprisingly the visit did not go well. The straight-laced social worker clearly disapproved of a house in disarray, and an apparently drunken friend collapsed on a bed. Hope's follow-up visit in an attempt to explain herself

---

21   The Melbourne matron is cited in 'Foundling Homes Doing a Great Job'. *Gippsland Times*, 21 January 1952, 6.

22   Oswald Barnett, *Is It Safe to Adopt a Baby? A Social Study.* Melbourne: Speciality Press, 1948.

23   For the lady volunteer, see 'Child Delinquency in Queensland. Parents Largely to Blame. Report in Parliament'. *Cairns Post,* 20 September 1951, 5.

to the social worker did not help. She struggled to 'manage a smile' but the social worker appeared unforgiving. 'She could almost imagine Miss Burbank thinking: "She protests too much; she's over-anxious. And that house was no place for a child!"' The intervention of a friend, already a mother, turned the tide, and the story ended with a phone call announcing that the much desired child was available.[24]

This fictional piece captures the shift which placed power so firmly in the hands of the social work profession. Given the rapidly growing demand, social workers were able to assert an expertise in selection and assessment based in practice knowledge derived primarily from the United States. Where they had once claimed to be expert at assessing the fitness of children for adoptive parents, now the focus shifted, with applicants rigorously assessed to provide security for the child. Central to this new professional practice was the concept of scientific 'matching', placing children with parents whose appearance, talents and social status were as similar as possible to those of their birth parents. Newspaper and magazine articles pleading with people to adopt were replaced by explanations of the procedures required, justifying the intrusion that this necessarily involved. Psychology was invoked to explain the restrictions in relation to age, income and religious affiliation that were part of the new regime. Answering criticism of the 'legal rigmarole' that adoption now involved, an Adelaide JP argued that as there were far more applicants than there were children to be adopted, 'the most suitable couple in the opinion of the court gets the preference'. Applicants could expect to be questioned 'in a kindly and friendly manner' in order to establish their ability to provide love and security for the child. Where, in the interwar years, single men and women had been encouraged to adopt, it now became a privilege restricted to respectable married couples. Most of these wanted to adopt children as early as possible, with infants moving into the new families as quickly as the law would allow.[25]

The applicants who survived the assessment process were enthusiastic about the new families which adoption had allowed them to create. 'We have no real failures', Melbourne's Women's Hospital almoner, Isabel Strahan declared. Her mailbag at Christmas was 'colossal', flooded with grateful messages from parents who had adopted, and, on occasions, from the children themselves. 'We didn't mind a bit', wrote a New South Wales mother. The assessment was no more intrusive than 'the sort of questions you

---

24   'The Latecomer'. *Australian Women's Weekly*, 28 August 1948, 11.
25   A.R. Chaffer JP to The Editor, 'Adopting A Child'. *Advertiser*, 28 October 1946, 10.

would be asked if you were taking out an insurance—and adopting a baby is much more important than that'. 'The world was changed for us', wrote a father from Western Australia in 1947, '... had I the means I would readily quadruple my adoptions'.[26]

A short story published in the *New Idea* in 1955 summarised the neat package that adoption had become. The single mother was 'frightened, disgraced, and unwanted' except by her parents who, having made 'hurried arrangements for the child's adoption', 'whisked' their daughter away for a new life. The adoptive parents collected the 'little bundle', providing it with a 'happy home with parents who really wanted to be parents'. 'For this mistake', the article concluded,

> there is every hope of a fine future. No complexes, psychological throwbacks, or handicaps... If Geoffrey the unwanted had been clutched and claimed by his natural mother, and had been nurtured even under reasonably good conditions, he would have been branded, to say the least, and his hopes for the future would have suffered accordingly.[27]

But some people were impatient with the procedures, and wanted to short-track their adoption applications. Press reports of abandoned babies were greeted by a rash of applications from parents offering to adopt. In the 1950s, a Melbourne newspaper estimated that only 30 per cent of adoptions were arranged by welfare agencies. Newspaper and magazine correspondents were prepared to introduce pregnant women to childless couples in the hope that they could make a 'satisfactory arrangement'. Following a tentative suggestion that she could solve the problem of a single mother by putting her in touch with a childless wife, *New Idea* problem page writer, 'Elizabeth Wyse', found herself overwhelmed by requests to help others make similar arrangements. For several months she became increasingly involved in bringing people together. In the end her editor instructed her to give up this role. Readers were urged instead to work through the Child Welfare Department or other authorised adoption agencies which 'have all the means of investigating every case and... the

---

26   Isabel Strahan: 'Would You Like To Own This Baby?' *Argus*, 20 July 1951, (Supplement): The Argus Magazine, 1; 'An Adoptive Mother, "We Adopted a Family"'. *Sunday Herald*, 19 April 1953, 12; and 'What's on your mind? A man gives his views on adoption'. *Australian Women's Weekly*, 9 August 1947, 27.
27   Colin Merrill, 'Just a Mistake'. *New Idea*, 16 February 1955, 7.

machinery for investigating the suitability of prospective parents and of children for adoption'.[28]

Cheryl Virginia Searle, who told her story to the Monash History of Adoption website, was adopted in 1943 through an informal arrangement. The woman who adopted her was working in munitions when the company's nurse offered her the chance to adopt a child. She visited the expectant mother in a maternity home several times before the baby was born. The final separation of mother and child was, however, traumatic. Having dressed the baby in clothes the adopting mother had prepared for her, the mother proudly displayed her to the other mothers in the home, but when the time came to part she 'went hysterical... it took two people to hold my birth mother... she just collapsed and my mum said that when she drove off with me she thought she was doing the wrong thing'. Nor was the separation complete at this time. Cheryl has a photo of herself with her birth family taken when she was two years old, although she is unsure how this meeting came about.

Patricia Brennan's adoption was arranged by nuns who approached a woman with five sons to see whether she was prepared to take on another child. 'What's another potato in the pot', the woman replied and went back to her home in the country to prepare for the baby's arrival, padding up so that neighbours would not suspect that the expected child was not her own.

Such informal arrangements were not illegal in most Australian jurisdictions. But with the increase in demand, stories began to circulate that in some cases substantial amounts of money were changing hands, reproducing in Australia the American market in children which local media commonly derided. Although the existence of such a black market was repeatedly denied, authorities admitted that it would be difficult to discover. The list of people wanting to adopt was 'enormous', the Matron of Melbourne's Berry Street home commented, confessing that she had 'strong suspicions' that some applicants were prepared to go outside the law. Accusations centred on 'certain private hospitals' where 'unscrupulous' medical or nursing staff used their position to locate infants available for adoption and to sell them on to parents anxious to adopt. While judges were required to automatically dismiss an adoption application in which money had changed hands, they were seldom in a position to discover that this had indeed been the case.[29]

---

28   'Have you a problem?' *New Idea*, 3 May 1950, 7; and 'Have you a problem?' *New Idea*, 18 October 1950, 6.

29   The Berry Street Matron is cited in 'Baby Traffic Probe is On'. *Argus*, 30 March 1950, 3. See also 'M.P. Says Babies Being Sold'. *Argus*, 29 March 1950, 1.

Journalists tried to deter people from making private arrangements, warning them that to go outside the approved channels was to 'encourage a sinister black market which the authorities are trying to stamp out'. Social workers warned that a mother who handed over her newborn baby to a stranger was just as likely to reappear years later to reclaim it. In 1956 the *New Idea* told the story of an infertile woman who became friends with a single mother and agreed to adopt her child. When the child was 17 her father found her, and so unsettled her that she left her adopted home, never to return. The article concluded that the mother who had adopted her 'never knew what became of her—whether she made good or went the way of her mother'. And children obtained in this way came with no guarantee as to quality. A baby adopted privately by a mother of four boys 'obsessed with adopting a girl', the magazine warned, had turned out to be 'not at all normal'.[30]

This message found its mark. A mother who had adopted, writing of her experiences in a Sydney newspaper, recalled that although she had friends who had adopted privately with no ill effects, she had decided to go through official channels. She was convinced that 'hospital matrons and doctors should not play God and hand out babies as favours just because people's gratitude made them feel important'.[31]

SEPARATING MOTHERS AND BABIES

If the demand for adoption was to be met through approved channels, then those channels had to increase the available supply. Services for pregnant single women were transformed. The older female refuges designed to shelter and reform were replaced by institutions which promised to help the young mother, but the price of that help was relinquishment. In public and private maternity hospitals, where staff dealt both with single women about to give birth and married women facing the pain of infertility or infant death, the pressure to see 'illegitimate' babies as 'unwanted' led to an increasing emphasis on adoption as the only possible solution. A 1941 *Australian Women's Weekly* article reported positively on the father who, after his wife lost her fourth child, 'adopted a three-days-old baby, [and] took mother and child to a private hospital. In a week's time, a proud mother will

---

30   The three articles cited here are 'Beware of the Show-off'. *New Idea*, 18 June 1958, 41; 'Baby'. *New Idea,* 4 January 1956, 21; and 'Have you a problem?' *New Idea,* 28 April 1954, 26.

31   'An Adoptive Mother, "We Adopted a Family"'. *Sunday Herald*, 19 April 1953, 12.

take home the babe she is nursing herself and not even her closest friends will know... '32

Management practices were introduced which minimised the mother's contact with her baby. Women who spent even a small part of their pregnancy in maternity homes were particularly under pressure, for each maternity home was linked to an approved adoption outlet and needed to keep the babies coming if the waiting lists were to be contained. From the first antenatal appointment, through the delivery to the signing of the relinquishment, the assumption that the child was destined for adoption was never questioned. Where mothers resisted they were accused of being unrealistic or selfish, and told that if they loved their baby they would give it away. If their levels of distress became too great they were restrained physically or chemically, further reducing their opportunity to exercise choice. In one Tasmanian maternity home the matron used the provisions of the Mental Deficiency Act to have mothers declared unfit to sign, and then to consent on their behalf. Social workers did not deny that mothers suffered dreadfully when they were separated from their children, but insisted that early separation was less painful than being forced to surrender the child later after struggling to support it and failing.

The children being transferred were even more effectively silenced. Perpetually infants, a blank slate on which new parents could draw their own image, the role of the adopted children was to be grateful for their 'rescue'. If someone complained that all was not well with a particular placement they would be told that an approach to 'the right people' would fix everything. The idea that adoption might be placing children in a situation worse than their mothers could have offered them was not to be countenanced.33

The growing shortage of babies for adoption saw attention turn to children previously classified as unadoptable because of mental or physical disabilities, or mixed racial origins. A 1951 appeal for adoptive parents for a fourteen year old girl who had been living for eleven years in a home for crippled children produced 63 replies. The increasing demand also raised the issue of institutionalised children who were not available for adoption. Their parents were depicted as selfish in not freeing their children to find a happier home, 'they cold-bloodedly wait for them to reach wage-earning age, when they can boost the family income'. A widely syndicated article published in 1954 celebrated parents who were prepared to take on the less than perfect

---

32   'Adoptions Help Cure War Heartaches. Foundlings and Orphans are More in Demand than Ever'. *Australian Women's Weekly,* 13 December 1941, 10.

33   See 'Outcast'. *New Idea,* 12 June 1931, 40.

child. 'Brave people who adopt defective children don't demand a gilt-edged guarantee, as if the child were a pure-bred calf... love blinds the new parents to any infirmity the child might have... They say they realise that if their own children had been born defective they would have had to put up with it. Some of them even feel that there is less risk in obtaining a baby "ready-made".[34]

It was this widening of the net that made more Indigenous children eligible for adoption. In earlier decades the principle of matching generally made them ineligible. First amongst the 'unadoptable' infants in the 1954 article was 'a dark-haired, dark-eyed, 12 months old baby girl, whose smiling eyes seemed to plead from her cot: "Please take me"'. The prospective parents who had taken a liking to the child were warned by the matron to prepare themselves for a 'bombshell', her mother was Aboriginal. Left for ten minutes to make their decision, the couple weighed their alternatives before declaring 'We'll take her'.

By the end of the 1950s, families were making private arrangements to adopt Aboriginal children as an act of benevolence. A 1957 article in the *Australian Women's Weekly* used the headline 'Mission to Mansion' to tell the story of a wealthy Melbourne family who had added two girls from the Northern Territory to their family of three (see Fig. 3.7). They saw this as an 'initial move for a nationwide assimilation of aborigines and half-bloods into the community'. After waiting for nine months for permission, they had decided to proceed on their own, bringing the children to Melbourne without the assurance of a legal adoption. 'Legality isn't everything', declared the mother who hoped to adopt; 'the love and care of not only parents, but brothers and sisters, often means more'. The girls were depicted as delighting in their new home, complete with 'a handsome electric organ... television... [and a] rooftop swimming-pool' in contrast to the filth and neglect they had left behind. Their parents' reluctance to sign relinquishment documents was cited as evidence of their disregard for the future welfare of their daughters.[35]

As the gap between buyers and sellers in the adoption market continued to widen, any parent of a child identified as adoptable who was reluctant to relinquish was increasingly condemned. A woman who wrote to the *New*

---

34 See 'Crippled Girl Happy in Her New Home'. *Advertiser*, 21 March 1951, 11; 'Tragedies of State Wards: Cold-blooded'. *Sunday Herald*, 9 July 1950, 6; and Ron Testro, 'Babies for the Brave'. *Argus Weekender*, 6 November 1954, 1.

35 'Mission to Mansion: Brand-new Family for Three Girls from Arnhem Land'. *Australian Women's Weekly*, 12 June 1957, 5.

Idea in 1958 regretting her decision to relinquish, and warning other single mothers not to make the same 'terrible mistake', attracted a torrent of criticism. 'Has she ever thought of the pangs suffered by women who, despite years of medical treatment and hoping and waiting, are still childless? Has she thought of the joy such a woman feels when, perhaps after a long waiting period, a baby becomes available for her to adopt?' 'She should find comfort in knowing she has brought great joy to some other woman and concentrate her own store of affection on her [future] husband and... children'.[36]

Some mothers were prepared to challenge the loss of their children in actions as well as words. The publicity which they attracted in the early 1950s undermined the confidence that legal adoption was meant to provide. Judges, perhaps less convinced about the rightness of adoption than politicians, weighed the claims to motherhood of the competing parties in their attempts to reach a decision that was in the best interests of the child. In Sydney, single mother Joan Murray was unfavourably compared with adopting mother Gloria Mace. Murray had attempted to reclaim her son nine weeks after signing the consent, but his adoptive parents refused to relinquish him, at one stage fleeing the state to move outside the court's jurisdiction. Murray fought the case through to the highest court of appeal, but after almost three years her battle was lost, without her ever having the opportunity to have any contact with her son (see Fig. 3.8). In Melbourne, Daphne Anderson was pitted against Dorothy Cole-Sinclair. Anderson's daughter, Susan, had been born as a result of an extra-marital affair and when Daphne was hospitalised because of mental illness, her estranged husband consented to the child's adoption. With the support of her family she contested the consent and, after an epic court struggle, the child left her adoptive parents' home and returned to live with her mother.

The publicity surrounding such trials called into question the assumptions on which adoption was based. Was a mother who adopted, the judges asked, as capable of loving and rearing a child as the woman who had given it birth? In the drama of the courtroom, lawyers acting for the adoptive parents set out to show that the mother separated by adoption had not developed the maternal feeling for the child demonstrated by the mother who adopted, while their opponents sought to depict their client as a loving mother who had been unjustly deprived of her child. Joan Murray's increasingly

---

36   See 'Help for the Unmarried Mother'. *New Idea*, 12 March 1958, 39; and 'She Pines for Baby who was Adopted'. *New Idea*, 30 April 1958. 38.

3.1 Children in state care at the Melbourne Orphanage, Brighton, [ca. 1920 – ca. 1930]. Photo by Spencer Shier. Some of these children would have been available for adoption, whereupon they would be freed from institutional life and cease to be a charge against the state.

State Library of Victoria, Pictures Collection, Image no. H2001.20/20, with permission.

3.2 Group of children outside Magill Orphans' Home, near Adelaide, South Australia, 1922. These children too would have been available for adoption.

State Library of South Australia PRG 280/1/28/254, with permission.

3.3 All types of babies were available to choose from. Matron with children at
Ngala Mothercraft Home and Training Centre, Jarrah Rd, South Perth, 1970–1979.
Photograph by Richard Woldendorp. State Library of Western Australia Image no.
b2466455.
With permission of the Library Board of Western Australia.

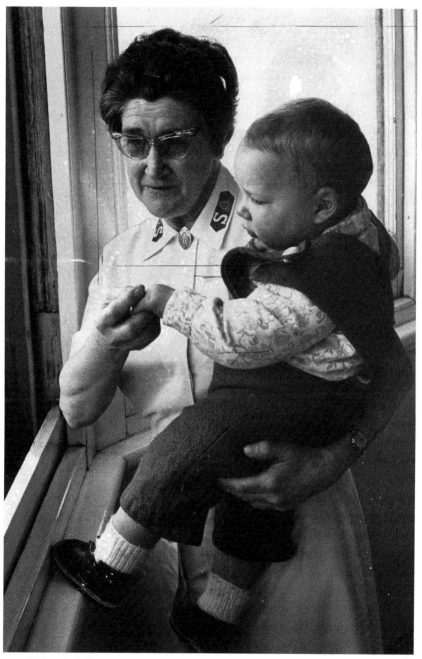

3.4 'When little girls are available no-one will look at the boys'. Brigadier Eva Stone, matron of The Haven, the Salvation Army's home for unmarried mothers and unwanted babies, with one of her unwanted charges, c. 1968. State Library of Victoria, Herald & Weekly Times Limited portrait collection, Image no. H38849/5727.

With permission Newspix (for Herald & Weekly Times Limited).

3.5 This poster advertising the seventeenth birthday of the Methodist Babies' Home in Melbourne (founded 1929) includes a parade of babies.
Stonnington History Centre, with permission.

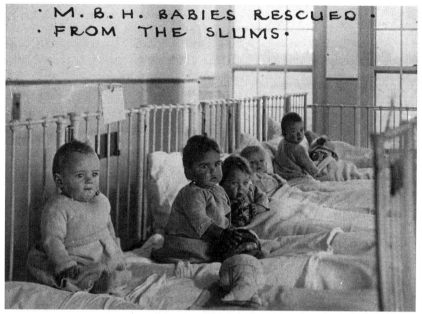

3.6 Lined up for selection at the Methodist Babies' Home, 1930s.
Connections Uniting Care with permission.

3.7 'Mission to Mansion': a Melbourne family with their adopted Aboriginal children,
c. 1958. One family member appears to have been added after the photo was taken. State
Library of Victoria, Herald & Weekly Times Limited portrait collection H38849/1115.
With permission Newspix (for Herald & Weekly Times Limited).

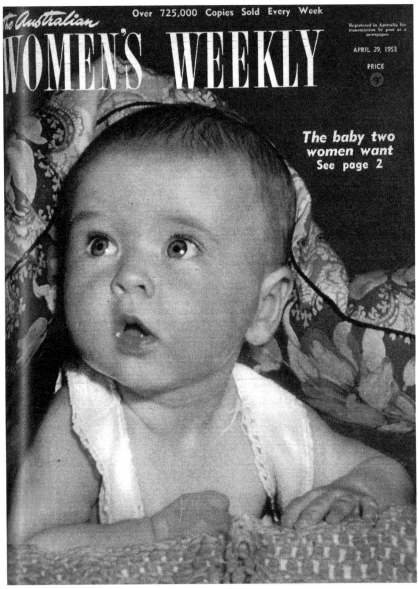

3.8 The baby two women wanted, *Australian Women's Weekly*, 29 April 1953. Single mother Joan Murray was unfavourably compared with adopting mother Mrs Gloria Mace as the two women battled each other in the courts when Miss Murray attempted to reclaim her child after signing an adoption consent.
With permission, *Australian Women's Weekly*.

frantic attempts to regain custody of her child were seen as evidence of her irrationality by lawyers who raked over her past behaviour in order to demonstrate her moral failings. As a young woman she had entertained men in her rooms, even though she was warned by the police that she was risking her character by doing so. During her pregnancy she had not looked forward to the birth, complaining to a social worker that she had 'had to give up jitter-bugging to have the baby'.[37]

By contrast, Mrs Mace's behaviour was read as evidence of the strong maternal affections she had developed. Explaining her reasons for fleeing with the child she said: 'I couldn't stop loving Peter because the law says so. I will always love him'. Although Murray's lawyer invoked her 'mother instinct' to explain her attempt to reclaim her child, the judges found Mace's claim more compelling, arguing that she was better positioned to provide Peter with a secure home. In a final attempt to see her child, Miss Murray went to the adoptive parents' home. As watching neighbours 'jeered' she was led away by her sister. 'They are defying a natural law', she said, struggling to accept her final defeat. 'They can't give away another person's baby'.[38]

There were several reasons why Daphne Anderson was able to succeed where Joan Murray had failed. She had never signed a consent and, with the support of her family, had the financial resources to provide for her child. She had cared for her daughter when she was born, and as soon as she was released from the hospital she had begun to fight for her return. Cole-Sinclair, by comparison, was a divorcee who, her former sister-in-law testified, had neglected and later deserted the children of her first marriage in order to pursue her relationship with her new husband. Much of the debate in the Victorian courts centred on the capacity to nurture of what was rather chillingly described as a 'permanent mother substitute', with the judges finally concluding that the bond of a mother to her child had to be stronger. Not only did Mr Justice Winneke conclude that 'blood is thicker than water', he went on to assert that 'the great majority of the population are brought up to believe that and do'. 'You have to look at the whole of the child's life, not merely the time it is young', the Chief Justice, Sir Edmund Herring added. 'We all know that as a child grows, and afterwards, a mother will always care

---

37   'Five Reasons for Mace Adoption. Submissions by Counsel'. *Sydney Morning Herald*, 25 August 1953, 4.

38   See 'Baby Dispute in Court. Bid for Adoption'. *Canberra Times*, 19 June 1953, 4; and 'Judge Gives Joan Murray's Child to the Maces'. *Canberra Times*, 22 September 1953, 1.

for it and love it'. Adoptive parents, by contrast, were comparative strangers whose commitment might not last over time.[39]

The expression of views like these brought cold comfort to parents who had believed themselves to be in secure possession of children whom no-one wanted, and the professionals who had encouraged them in this belief. 'Hundreds of parents are asking: are our babies safe?' a Melbourne newspaper heading declared. The reaction was swift: the law must be reformed. The judges had erred, a Melbourne columnist argued, in paying much attention 'to the natural feelings of the mother for her child... social workers who have seen thousands of these cases do not seem to be so deeply impressed as judges by the bond between mother and child. They think first of the infant's security'. The welfare of children, it was argued, was best served by early and secure relinquishment. An 'unnatural mother' who sought to stand in the way of her child's future should be denied the right to withhold her consents, as should other 'irresponsible parents' who were depriving their children 'of the benefits of good homes and a fair chance in life'.[40]

The Adoption Acts passed by most of the states during the 1960s were in large part a response to these demands. In 1960 the Commonwealth Attorney-General Garfield Barwick proposed that the states should pass uniform adoption laws. Barwick's first concern was with the legalities of adoption, matters such as jurisdiction and domicile. But consent was also an issue. Barwick's office had received 'a large number of letters' from people wanting to adopt children whose parents refused to consent to their adoption. State welfare officers advised that in some cases parental consent should be 'dispensed with more easily than at present'. A meeting of attorneys-general showed fleeting sympathy for 'poor parents who will not yield up to the rich adopter', but in general there was little concern for parents' rights. The Model Bill drawn up by Barwick's department as a basis for state legislation spelt out a number of cases in which the court could override parental objections to adoption, including failure to discharge the obligations of a guardian to the child. It also specified that parents who had signed adoption orders had only thirty days in which to change their minds, after which the order could not be revoked. In the state laws which were passed in the following

---

39   'Mother of Adopted Girl asks Judge to Rescind Order'. *Age*, 9 February 1955, 8; 'Bond with Mother Closer, Says Q.C'. *Age*, 10 February 1955, 5; 'Counsel Says Refusal to End Adoption Right'. *Age*, 11 February 1955, 3.

40   'Hundreds of Parents are Asking: Are Our Babies Safe? The Fry Case'. *Argus*, 15 May 1954, 11; and Geoffrey Hutton, 'Closing Loopholes in State Adoption Laws'. *Age*, 23 June 1955, 2.

decade, revocation periods were clearly defined and secrecy provisions were strengthened, so that no more 'whose baby?' cases could occur. [41]

Senior social workers were more aware of the pressures driving adoption, and more concerned to spell out the rights of mothers separated by adoption. In the late 1950s a pamphlet published by the Victorian Council of Social Service declared that a social worker's duties to 'the natural mother' included help with emotional stress, accommodation, employment and financial aid, together with medical and hospital care and plans 'for her own and her child's future'—though the assumption remained that adoption was the preferred outcome for the child. It seems that the ideal practice recommended here was not generally followed in interactions between social workers and mothers.

Take the case of 'financial aid'. Various forms of assistance could have been accessed by single mothers, before and after birth. All mothers were eligible for the Commonwealth 'baby bonus', paid immediately after birth. Unemployment, sickness and special benefits were available, and from 1964, Commonwealth-subsidised state payments for mothers who were ineligible for the widow's pension. These were not generous payments, but with family support they may have been enough to live on. But the 2012 Senate inquiry reported that the mothers it heard had not been informed about available financial support. It cited the example of Rosemary West, who founded the Council of Single Mothers and their Children to fight discrimination against single mothers:

> For me, the penny dropped when I was pregnant in 1962 and asked the hospital social worker about social security benefits. She told me that I had broken the rules, and there was nothing for me. Girls like me were threatening the institution of marriage, she said, and if I cared for my child I would give it up.[42]

---

41   The long process of achieving more or less uniform state adoption laws is documented in a series of files held in the records of the Attorney-General's Department in the Commonwealth Archives: 'Possibility of Commonwealth Legislation Re Uniform Processes of Adoption'. NAA A432 1958/3087; 'Uniform Adoption Legislation. Material prepared for conference'. NAA A432 1961/2241 Part 2. The various state Adoption Acts are Queensland 1964, Victoria 1964, ACT 1965, NSW 1965, South Australia 1966–1967, and Tasmania 1968.

42   *The Service of Adoption.* 'Issued by the Victorian Council of Social Service for the guidance of those interested in adoption', not dated but published before 1960. The report of the Senate inquiry into forced adoption devotes a long chapter to the 'Commonwealth role: social security and benefits system': Rosemary West is quoted in paragraph 5.57.

The Adoption Acts of the 1960s met a mixed reaction from the social work profession. Leading social workers generally welcomed the legislation and the practices it mandated. In 1966 the Victorian Branch of the Association of Social Workers issued a policy statement in response to the passage of the new act which whole-heartedly endorsed the first principle of the legislation: that adoption should operate in the interests of the child. The policy statement began with the proposition that 'The primary purpose [of adoption] is to enable the child whose parents cannot keep him, to gain the love, care, security, status, and opportunities he needs as an established member of another family'; the needs of couples who wanted children were placed firmly second to the needs of the child. The statement also spelt out the rights of the 'biological mother':

> To a full explanation of the implications of consenting to her child's adoption; to decide whether or not her child is to be adopted; to decide whether she sees the child before placement; to medical information about the child; to know the outcome of plans for the child; to re-involvement if the child cannot be adopted; to legal protection against re-involvement after an Adoption Order is made.

But it is clear from the reports of mothers who experienced adoption in Victoria at this period that social workers at the agency level did not always honour these principles in their practice.[43]

In New South Wales the pattern was the same. When the new Adoption Act was enacted, in 1967, the Council of Social Work of New South Wales and the Australian Medical Association organised a seminar to explain its implications for adoption practice. Again, the leaders of the profession endorsed the regulatory principles involved, including provisions intended to protect the rights of mothers separated by adoption. On the matter of consent, for example, a social work administrator from the Department of Child Welfare endorsed a regulation intended to guarantee that when a mother signed a consent form she did so with full knowledge and without duress. Social workers were now required to sign a document declaring that before witnessing a mother's signature they had explained the full effect of that signature, and given the mother 'ample opportunity' to read the consent form. Again, reports from mothers suggest that the regulation had little immediate impact on practice.

---

43 'Adoption: A Policy Statement'. Australian Association of Social Workers, Victorian Branch, 1966.

The report from the discussion session at the conclusion of this seminar makes it clear that people working at the coalface found aspects of the new act intrusive and damaging to practices which they valued. 'Rapid adoption' was a case in point. Mothers in New South Wales would now have thirty days in which to change their minds about giving up their children. Speakers from the floor regretted this innovation. Some of the most successful adoptions in New South Wales had been achieved by the practice of placing newborn babies immediately into the care of mothers adopting them. With the thirty day rule this would no longer be possible.[44]

For all the talk about the rights of mothers and of adopted children, the effect of the 1960s adoption Acts was to sever every connection between mother and child. Adoption records were sealed. The legal claims of adopting parents were strengthened. The baby market was refigured in the interests of consumers.

If past morality was to be a measure of the ability to mother, Joan Murray's legal counsel had warned, 'a large proportion of young Australian women would not have the right to claim their children born out of wedlock'. Under the amended adoption laws his prophecy was fulfilled. More than twenty years were to pass before another generation of adopted children came to maturity and began to assert their rights to information about their origins. In so doing they created a space for mothers to speak of the impact losing their babies had had on their lives.[45]

---

44 *Adoption services in New South Wales: Proceedings of a seminar held on Friday, 3rd February, 1967.* Published by the New South Wales Department of Child Welfare and Social Welfare.
45 'Baby Case Judgment Reserved'. *Advertiser*, 3 December 1954, 3.

CHAPTER 4

SPEAKING TRUTH TO POWER

I am a girl of 19 and am expecting a baby in early January. My boyfriend, the baby's father, and I cannot get married and have decided it is best to have the baby adopted. Could you give me the names of any homes where I may go until the baby is born? Where do we apply for the papers for adoption? Is it possible to have the adoption arranged without our parents being told? They do not know about my condition.

"Little Mother," Qld.

Louise Hunter published this letter in her advice column for teenagers in the *Australian Women's Weekly*, October 1958. Her reply was brief and to the point, directing the young woman to the two establishments in Brisbane where she could 'await the birth' of her baby, and stressing that she should tell her parents immediately.[46]

In the decades after the Second World War, women's journals carried a steady flow of advice about adoption. Unmarried mothers were generally advised that adoption was the best option for themselves and for their babies. Women wanting to adopt were told to 'look upon the child as their very own, as indeed he is', and not to inquire about the child's parents: 'The less you know of the child's biological parents the better. For your own peace of mind, they should not know anything of you'. Social workers and other professionals presented adoption as the ideal solution to the double problems of infertility and illegitimacy. A pamphlet issued in New South Wales told intending parents that:

---

46   Louise Hunter, 'Here's Your Answer'. *Australian Women's Weekly*, 22 October 1958, 47.

Adoption is our society's method for creating families for children who need a permanent home which will offer them happiness and security. These children will have needs to be met and love to give to those able to fulfil the challenging, but rewarding role of Adopting Parents. At the same time, adoption provides a means for parents unable to look after their children making a worthwhile plan for their future.[47]

Sixty years later attitudes and understandings have changed. In 2005 a parliamentary inquiry into adoption in Australia found

a general lack of support for adoption... in most of the state and territory welfare departments which are responsible for processing all adoption applications. The lack of support ranged from indifference to hostility.

Since 2005 political condemnation of adoption has increased, culminating in March 2013 when the Commonwealth parliament formally apologised to 'all those who have experienced pain and suffering through adoption'.[48]

This chapter tells how understandings of adoption have changed, from uncomplicated approval to the point where, in the bitter words of a mother who adopted, 'adoption is now a dirty word'. It charts the growth of groups of adoptees and mothers separated by adoption, first as self-help groups, then as political activists lobbying to gain access to their birth records. It shows how the language of protest changed, from claiming civil rights to citing grievances based in 'pain and suffering'. It shows how this change mirrored the language of medical professionals and social workers, and became the language of reporters and script writers. And how, for some mothers, the opening of their adoption records revealed histories of coercion

---

47   For an example of advice to single mothers, see 'Surrender her Baby? The unmarried mother's problem... should she?' *Australian Women's Weekly*, 8 September 1954, 26. 'Medico' advised women wanting to adopt in the *Australian Women's Weekly*, 10 May 1947, 40. The New South Wales pamphlet, *Adoption in New South Wales: A Pamphlet to help Parents' Thinking about Adoption*, is held in the Halse Rogers papers, Mitchell Library (State Library of NSW) ML1153/62 3 (4).

48   The 2005 inquiry, by the House of Representatives Standing Committee on Family and Human Services, produced a report to the Commonwealth Parliament, *Overseas Adoption in Australia; Report of the Inquiry into Adoption of Children from Overseas,* November 2005. For the views of parents who adopted see the 'Aims of National Adoption Awareness Week', 2012, at http://www. adoptionawarenessweek.com.au/Home. To see and hear Julia Gillard deliver the apology go to http://www.abc.net.au/news/2013-03-21/gillard-delivers-apology-to-victims-of-forced-adoption/.

that could only be redressed by a public acknowledgement of how they had been wronged. [49]

RIGHTS FOR THE PARTIES TO ADOPTION

At the fortieth birthday celebrations of the Council of Single Mothers and their Children, Sandy Fitts recalled a meeting with the Commonwealth Minister for Social Services. She dated her memory by the age of her child: 'my new baby is gurgling in the white wicker carry basket, so it must be around April 1969'. Sandy Fitts and Rosemary West were meeting the minister to persuade him that 'never-married single mothers' should enjoy the same rights and benefits as widows and deserted wives.

They met in a wood-panelled room in an office attached to St. Paul's Anglican Cathedral in Melbourne. The two young mothers put their case in social justice terms: the children of single mothers have the same needs as those of widows. The minister listened politely, then turned to ask the opinion of an older woman sitting by his side—the matron of the Anglican maternity home. She replied that 'single mothers are better handled at State level, because the State is closer to the problems; that's where the adoption services are managed, and this is what happens to most babies of unmarried mothers'. Fitts and West protested: 'that wouldn't be the case if mothers could choose more freely'. But they could tell that the minister's views tallied with the matron's.

The Council of Single Mothers and their Children was newly formed in 1969—'the first single mothers' group in the world run by single mothers'. Founder Rosemary West was a student activist and journalist, and she conceived the group as 'something that's a cross between student action and a trade union'. The group understood their mission as 'creating a paradigm shift', from viewing 'unmarried/single mothers' as 'bad, mad or sad' to recognising them as 'caring mothers and good citizens'. In concrete terms they set out to abolish illegitimacy and to get the widows' pension extended to all single mothers. To achieve this they wrote articles for newspapers and women's magazines, established a mailing list, put out a newsletter, gave talks to professionals, students and church groups, and wrote and distributed 'Information Sheets' for single mothers and the nurses and social workers whom they dealt with—'the first welfare rights statements produced by a self-help group'. They lobbied politicians for

---

49   Cited in Denise Cuthbert, 'Mothering the "Other"'. *Balayi* 1(1) (2000): 35.

financial support, and welfare agencies for moral and political support, with increasing success.[50]

The public appearance of a group of single mothers as political agitators was symptomatic of a vast sea-change in Australian attitudes to sex—and so to unmarried motherhood, illegitimacy, and ultimately to family. The shift was from concealment to acknowledgement, the making public of previously private intimacies. Sex became a fit subject for men and women to talk about, in language which affirmed the pleasures of sex without the responsibilities of procreation. Germaine Greer's feminist manifesto *The Female Eunuch* was published in 1970, and her demand that women should enjoy sex for its own sake was widely discussed in the Australian media. In November 1972 the Packer family launched *Cleo* magazine, a mainstream publication aiming amongst other things to inform women about those same pleasures of sex; its first print run sold out in two days. The contraceptive pill had been available to married women since the early 1960s, but it was not until the late 1960s that doctors began regularly prescribing it for unmarried women. In 1973 it became available on the Pharmaceutical Benefits Scheme. From 1967 to 1974 sales of oral contraceptives in New South Wales almost doubled.[51]

At the same time the language of rights was heard on all sides in parliament and the press. Taking their cue from international struggles, workers went on strike for workers' rights, consumers demanded consumer rights, Aborigines claimed land rights as indigenous citizens. Militant feminists added new demands for personal and bodily autonomy to the civil and legal rights that their mothers had pursued for decades. The right to abortion became a rallying point, rousing fierce opposition and winning political and legal support; legislation in South Australia in 1970 and legal judgements in Victoria in 1969 and New South Wales in 1972 effectively authorised doctors to carry out abortions in the interests of their patients' mental and physical health. In this political climate the lobbying of the Council of Single Mothers and their Children fell on fertile ground. In 1973 the Whitlam government introduced a supporting mothers' pension which included single mothers, and in 1974 the Hamer government in Victoria passed legislation abolishing the practice of stamping the birth certificates of

50   See accounts by Sandy Fitts, Rosemary West, and Jo Clancy in *The Council of Single Mothers and their Children: Ruby Anniversary: The History of CSMS Achievements.* http://www.csmc.org.au/?q=history

51   Michelle Arrow, 'Public Intimacies: Revisiting the Royal Commission on Human Relationships (1974–1977)'. Conference paper given at *Histories of Motherhood in Australia*, State Library of New South Wales, 29 September 2011.

the children of single mothers with the word 'illegitimate'. Most of the other states followed in the next few years. Neither of these achievements can be solely credited to the CMSC, but their input was significant.

The immediate consequence of these changes was a decline in the numbers of babies available for adoption. In June 1973, Ms Pam Roberts, a senior social worker and chairman of the New South Wales Standing Committee on Adoption, reported that the outlook was bleak.

> The situation in the field at the moment is that the number of babies being born and surrendered for adoption has reduced dramatically in the last 6–8 months. Probably reasons are more knowledge of contraception, more termination of pregnancy, more mothers retaining custody. At the same time there are larger numbers of prospective parents applying.

Her committee was concerned at the growing waiting lists for adoption; 'the waiting time for a boy has doubled in eight months'. The adoption agency run by the Salvation Army had already been driven 'out of business'.[52]

The agencies dealing in adoptions suffered so acutely in New South Wales because they had been enjoying a boom in supply specific to that state. From 1969 the number of New South Wales babies available for adoption had been inflated by changes to women's access to abortion. Although abortion had long been illegal in Australia, it was readily available to those who knew where to go and who to pay. The 1969 Victorian ruling allowing medically-approved abortions led in that state to an immediate decline in police prosecutions of abortionists, and in births to unmarried mothers. In New South Wales the police reacted to the abortion debate by cracking down on the abortionists, closing their businesses and making it almost impossible to get an abortion. Births to single mothers increased by 150 per cent between 1969 and 1972, and adoptions rose at a similar rate, peaking at 4500 a year. With the New South Wales judiciary ruling in favour of therapeutic abortion in August 1972, abortion again became widely available, and numbers of adoptions fell rapidly to 1500 in 1976, a 70 per cent decline. In Victoria the decline began from 1970, with totals falling from about 2000 in that year to 1700 in 1973 to about 1000 in 1976. Across Australia numbers continued to fall away, from nearly 10,000 in 1972 to about 3000 in 1980, and to a few hundred annually today.[53]

---

52   Pam Roberts' report is held in the Halse Rogers papers, Mitchell Library as above.
53   The 'peak' in New South Wales adoptions is explained in an article by J. Kraus,

The wider social and political changes of the decade also played a role in this decline. From the early seventies women's magazines carried sympathetic articles about mothers who chose to keep their babies, like the 'business girl' Elizabeth who signed the adoption order but changed her mind because

> I'd spend the rest of my life wondering and worrying about her—wondering whom she had ended up with, worrying about what sort of life she was living. (See Fig. 4.2)

The Commonwealth pension granted to unmarried mothers in July 1973 made it easier for them to keep their children, both in the meagre support it offered, and in the assurance that it gave to their families that single motherhood was socially acceptable. A woman who was pregnant and unmarried in the early 1970s remembered:

> So I then went home for Christmas and told my mother that I was pregnant. And, I said that I would have to have the baby adopted and she said to me—'Why?' [Laughing] Thank God for mothers who ask questions, because in fact I hadn't... I mean, it was still very early days, obviously, but I actually hadn't had... nobody asked the question... So, that actually changed it, and I came back to Melbourne and continued with the pregnancy.

By 1975 about 80 per cent of the single mothers giving birth at Melbourne's Royal Women's Hospital were choosing to take home their babies, up from 35 per cent in 1969.[54] Private adoption agencies were going out of business across the nation.

'Historical Context of the Adoption "Crisis" in New South Wales'. *Australian Social Work*, 29(4) (1976): 19–25. Adoption statistics have been published by the Australian Government in two series, *Adoptions Australia* 1982–1989, and *Adoptions Australia*, from 1990. Reports from 1997 onwards are online at http://www.aihw.gov.au/adoptionspublications/

54   'The Story of Elizabeth' is in the *Australian Women's Weekly*, 5 April 1972, 6. Margaret McDonald made the plea in her address 'Adoption—the Long View Forward'. In McDonald (ed.), *Has Adoption a Future*, 7–22. The mother who kept her baby, and the details about adoptions at the Royal Women's Hospital, Melbourne, are included in the RWH's submission to the Senate inquiry into forced adoption. Parliament of Australia: Senate Community Affairs References Committee, *Commonwealth contribution to former forced adoption policies and practices*, February 2012. http://www.aph.gov.au/Parliamentary_Business/Committees/Senate_Committees?url=clac_ctte/completed_inquiries/2010-13/comm_contrib_former_forced_adoption/index.htm

To read the submissions to this inquiry, go to http://www.aph.gov.au/Parliamentary_Business/Committees/Senate_Committees?url=clac_ctte/completed_

JIGSAW AND LEGAL REFORM

The long term decline in adoption led to changes in the practice of social work. Adoption had been an important part of the work done by social workers in the 1960s, for many the most satisfying part. A social work educator remembered the pleasure of finding the right baby for the right couple: 'You are giving... something very precious and desired to people who are selected for their good qualities'.[55] But as the supply of babies declined, leading social workers recognised that their professional practice would have to change.

The First Australian Conference on Adoption in February 1976 was organised in large part as a response to the crisis in supply. International speakers told the conference that adoption practice needed to move its focus from babies to children with special needs. American Kay Donley was blunt about the impact of this change on the relationship of social workers and adoptive parents.

> The *child* is the client in adoption. Everyone says that of course but I *mean* it. You must be wary of the siren songs you sing yourself. The family you are currently working with may be your own dream come true in terms of being super parents [but]... Keep in mind you are being seduced—by them, by yourself. Your job is the placement of children, the finding and sustaining of families for youngsters, never the locating of children for those lovely people.

The director of the New South Wales Catholic Welfare Commission echoed this sentiment: 'The would-be adoptive parents have the right to be treated with respect and justice, but they do not have the right to receive a child'.

Other speakers stressed the need for social workers to be involved not only in the placement of children, but in a long-term role post adoption. Cliff Picton, a social work academic and organiser of the conference, explained that this meant a rethinking of the role of adoptive parents. The legal fiction that their new child became 'as if born' to them concealed the reality that their relationship had to be constructed, and many parents needed the ongoing support of a social worker to achieve this. 'Traditional adoption practice' was not a good basis for such a relationship; Picton recognised

---

inquiries/2010-13/comm_contrib_former_forced_adoption/submissions.htm The RWH submission is Submission 400, 83–84.

55   Cliff Picton was interviewed by J. Bowen for the ABC *Hindsight* program in 2011. See 'Tangled Web: The Silence of Consent'. http://www.abc.net.au/rn/hindsight/ stories/2011/3164428.htm

that for most parents: 'if I had an adoption problem the last person I would discuss it with would be my social worker'.[56]

Parents who had adopted were present at the conference, both in the audience and on the platform. A radical stream within social work, and especially in Victoria, understood their professional duty as creating social change by transforming their 'clients' into active, self-motivating 'consumers' of welfare. Victorian social workers had assisted with the formation of the Council of Single Mothers and their Children in 1969, and had worked closely with adoptive parents' organisations during the great influx of Vietnamese 'orphans' in 1975. Speakers representing the CSMC and Australian Society for Intercountry Aid (Children) offered a profound challenge to mainstream practice, declaring that

> the client, consumer and citizens groups… are neither more nor less important than the professional agencies—but they declare their right to be equal and will continue to stress this until all sections of the profession recognise it.

Other parent groups who were not represented on the platform protested less politely about the tyranny of the social work profession. In the months after the conference the president of the group Rights for Adoptive Parents demanded of the Department of Social Welfare that 'in future social workers who are childless and/or unmarried should have little influence and no authority in adoption matters'. RAP was far from satisfied with the social workers' response that 'we find families for children, not children for families'.[57]

The conference promoted the growth of activism amongst a group whose interests in adoption were very different from those of the adoptive parents. The cause that united them was the reform of adoption legislation to open their original birth records to enquiry—reform that had to happen state by state. Jigsaw was the first adoptee self-help group in Australia. Meetings in early 1976 in Melbourne and Sydney attracted both adoptees and 'natural

---

56   The papers by Kay Donley, Fr J. Devoran (the Director of NSW Catholic Welfare Council), and Cliff Picton are published in *Proceedings of the First Australian Conference on Adoption, 15–20 February, 1976*, edited by Cliff Picton. [Clayton, Vic]: Committee of the First Australian Conference on Adoption, 1976.

57   Phillip Mendes wrote about radical social workers in 'The History of Social Work in Australia: A Critical Literature Review'. *Australian Social Work*, 58(2) (2005): 121–131. Rosemary Calder and Jo Murray gave papers on the role of consumer groups to the first Australian conference on adoption, see Picton (ed.), *Proceedings of the First Australian Conference on Adoption*. Marian Quartly has written about these events in an article '[W]e find families for children, not children for families'. *Social Policy and Society*, 11(3) (2012): 415–427.

mothers' anxious to make contact with their children separated by adoption. Contacts at the conference spread the word, and by September 1976 Jigsaw had 39 members in four states: Victoria, New South Wales, Queensland and South Australia; about two thirds of these were adoptees, and one third 'natural parents'. By October the banner of the association's newsletter embraced them all:

> JIGSAW represents the interests of those adoptees, natural parents and others seeking to establish their connections or to make contact with persons in the lost world of adoption.

The group operated both as a service helping people to search for lost relatives, and as a pressure group on politicians and administrators. Over the next five years it achieved over 500 reunions in Victoria, despite the fact that seeking knowledge of the other party to the adoption was illegal under existing legislation. Publicising these reunions proved a useful political tactic, as well as a way of growing the association's membership.[58]

Action came first in Victoria. Jigsaw's call for law reform met with a prompt and sympathetic response from the Hamer government. In November 1976 the attorney-general Haddon Storey asked the parliamentary Statute Law Revision Committee to consider whether the adoption law should be changed to open adoptees' birth certificates to public access. Over the next two years the committee met with representatives from adoption agencies and hospitals, and from self-help groups: Jigsaw, the Council of Single Mothers and their Children, and adoptive parents. Their report, finally delivered in October 1978, dismayed Jigsaw members. It recommended that the law should be changed 'to permit an adopted person to obtain a copy of his or her original birth certificate', but only with very restrictive qualifications. Counselling was required before an application could be made; and access was subject to the decision of a judge, and the consent of the 'natural mother'. Access was limited to adoptees; the committee specifically recommended that 'a natural parent should not have a right to identifying information about an adopted child'.[59]

---

58 A full run of the *ALMA/Jigsaw Newsletters*, 1976–1986, is held in the Jigsaw Collection, JIGSAW 104/41 Box 18, series 18/19, in University of Melbourne Archives. Marie Meggitt's 1991 Monash MA thesis, 'The Role of Self Help in the Development of Public Policy', examines the making of the Victorian 1984 Adoption of Children Act.

59 See *Report from the Statue Law Revision Committee upon Access to Information Concerning Adoptions*. Victorian Parliament, 1978, 11.

It seems likely that the conservative conclusions of the SLRC report echoed the opinion of most of the agencies and hospitals, and certainly of the adoptive parents' groups. But Jigsaw's arguments fell on more fertile ground amongst welfare administrators and leading social workers. Robert Bender, co-founder and chair of Jigsaw Victoria, was invited in mid-1976 to join the Victorian Standing Committee on Adoption, and his submissions were well received. The committee was formed after the First Australian Conference on Adoption in Sydney, in part to organise a second conference in Melbourne, and 'the rights of adoptees' became a central concern in planning the conference. One of the lead speakers was John Triseliotis, an academic whose research had supported the passage in 1975 of English legislation opening the sealed birth records. His address in May 1978 argued that the rights of adoptees to access their own records could be met without any embarrassment to parents. Triseliotis' paper was reported positively in the Australian press.[60]

Haddon Storey remained sympathetic to the cause of adoption law reform. Months before the tabling of the SLRC report he was working to set up a second inquiry independent of parliament. In August 1978 he established an Adoption Legislation Review Committee, to report on 'the present law of adoption in Victoria'. Members included a parent who had adopted, a 'natural mother' from the Council of Single Mothers and their Children, and the chairman of Jigsaw.[61]

The Adoption Legislation Review Committee reported back nearly five years later, in March 1983, to a Labor ministry. Those years saw great changes in the media's presentation of adoption issues. Human interest pieces in newspapers and journals moved from feel-good tales of happy adoptive families to harrowing stories of the suffering of adoptees unable to discover their biological origins, and mothers unable to contact their lost children. Again the *Australian Women's Weekly* mirrored the shifting views. In 1976 readers were encouraged to debate the issue of relinquishment in its columns, producing a 'flood' of letters including many from mothers regretting their decision to allow their babies to be adopted. In 1977 a 'Reader's Story' took the form of a letter written 'to my natural mother' by an adoptee trying to

---

60   For John Triseliotis' paper see *Current Concerns and Alternatives for Child Placement and Parenting: Proceedings of the Second Australian Conference on Adoption, Melbourne May 1978*, edited by Cliff Picton. [Melbourne]: Committee of the Second Australian Conference on Adoption, 1979.

61   *Report*, Adoption Legislation Review Committee (ALRC), Victoria. Melbourne: Department of Community Welfare Services, March 1983.

make contact. In the same year an article praised the efforts of an Aboriginal mother to ensure that Aboriginal children were fostered and adopted only with Aboriginal families. In 1980 an editorial carried the plea of 'one of our readers who has been trying to find her biological mother most of her life':

> If you are female, about 70 years, who bore a daughter on 3/9/1930 and gave her up for adoption at the Methodist Babies Home, Camberwell, Vic, a few months later, then I may be your daughter. I can be contacted through Adoption Jigsaw WA…

The *Weekly*'s disenchantment with adoption peaked in 1981 with an article entitled 'Needs a "Miracle" to Keep Her Child'. It told the story of an adoptee, now a young single mother, who was unwillingly preparing to give up her child for adoption. In the words of the *Weekly* 'the long emotional search for her [own] mother has left [her] unable to cope with her own child'. Only the knowledge that her lost mother cared for her would give her the strength to take her child back and try again. And the *Weekly* provided that miracle. Two weeks later the journal reported that the adoptee had met with her birth family and 'found her identity at last'. 'Now her many years of uncertainty are over and she looks forward to a happy life with her baby'.[62]

In Victoria the very existence of the Adoption Legislation Review Committee was a catalyst for change; the professionals who gave evidence found themselves defending practices that they had previously taken as unquestionable. The committee's public consultations around Victoria were widely reported in the press, and Jigsaw's reunion program provided a running supply of human interest stories. At times there was close co-operation between pro-reform activists and committee members. When the Liberal government declined to make public an interim report from the ALRC, its chairman Bill Davey presented the report to a conference on adoption organised in 1980 by the National Council for Single Mothers and their Children, ensuring its wide circulation.[63]

By the time the final report was presented to parliament in June 1983 the Jigsaw activists could claim that they had persuaded public opinion to support

---

62 See *Australian Women's Weekly*, 4 February 1976, 36–38; 10 March 1976, 11–13; 2 February 1977, 102; 'Being Black and Together—That's Beautiful!' 25 May 1977, 45; 'Editorial'. 11 June 1980, 3; 6 May 1981, 6; and 27 May 1981, 6.

63 Marie Meggitt reports this in her thesis, 'The Role of Self Help in the Development of Public Policy', 105–106.

the idea of opening the closed records.[64] The committee's recommendation of full access for all adoptees, without qualification, proved less controversial than their proposals for more open and flexible forms of adoption and guardianship which retained ties with the natural parents. It was intended that these ties would be secured by 'conditional consents', agreements between adopting and natural parents made before consent was given to adopt, and authorised by the court at the time of the adoption. These proposals came not from the adoptee community but from progressive elements within the social work profession, who were already embracing more flexible forms of permanency planning and open adoption as the way forward.[65]

The legislation based on the ALRC report came before parliament in May 1984. The Labor government was open to social change, and Pauline Toner, the responsible minister, was absolutely committed to the reforms. She worked strenuously to present a Bill that the opposition would accept, using consultations, briefings, and pre-release of information to the other parties. The principle of full access to birth information seems to have had Opposition support. The fiercest debates were around conditional consent. It became apparent that lobbying from adoptive parents' associations had persuaded conservative politicians to reject any measures empowering birth parents in the adoption process. In the end it proved impossible to get the Bill through without robbing the conditional consent provisions of legal purchase, and adoptee access to birth records was qualified by requiring adoptees to undergo counselling before receiving their records.[66]

The 1984 Adoption Act was nevertheless a great victory for the Jigsaw adoptee community. Branches in other states took heart and regrouped to carry on the fight. In Western Australia the Jigsaw journal carried the headline LIGHTS! LIGHTS! LIGHTS!

> All those Western Australians who still suffer from the traumas of adoption—share the excitement with us! The *lights of liberation* are burning brightly in at least one Australian State.

The editorial went on to urge members to take their demands for legislative change to their local politicians; 'they are waiting to hear from you'. But

---

64 ALRC *Report*, 92.
65 For example see papers by John Booth and Terry O'Mara, in Oxenbury (ed), *Changing Families.*
66 Meggitt's thesis, 'The Role of Self Help in the Development of Public Policy', explores the role of Pauline Toner, p. 109 ff. The Victorian Adoption Act 1984 can be accessed at http://www.austlii.edu.au/au/legis/vic/consol_act/aa1984107/

change would not come until 1987 in Western Australia, and years later in the other states.[67]

ARMS AND THE PAIN OF SEPARATION

Single mothers were less enthusiastic about the Victorian reforms. The Council of Single Mothers and their Children had worked alongside Jigsaw throughout the campaign, organising public meetings, lobbying individual politicians—and in the last days of the parliamentary debate, sitting through long sessions and buttonholing politicians to strengthen their resolve and make clear to them the meaning of devious amendments. But with the watering down of the conditional consent provisions, the act did little to change the status of birth parents within adoption. The Bill had never looked to include birth parents alongside adoptees as parties with rights to access information.[68]

By 1984 there was another player in the reform lobby—the Association of Relinquishing Mothers. The Third Australian Conference on Adoption was held in Adelaide in May 1982. Its theme, *Changing Families*, echoed the research findings of the Australian Institute of Family Studies, that the nuclear family of two parents and two or three children was no longer the norm in Australian society; that two-generational families, 'blended' families and especially one parent families should be accepted as valid ways of nurturing children. One session addressed the needs of mothers denied the right to nurture their children, in language inflected with Freudian theory: ambivalence, guilt, denial, repression, unresolvable grief. Women spoke from the floor about their own experiences, often for the first time.[69]

In the last session of the conference the Sydney activist Judy McHutchinson read a statement on behalf of the 'relinquishing mothers' present, announcing the formation of the Australian Relinquishing Mothers Sisterhood.

---

67 Ron J. Elphick's *The Adoption Jigsaw*, Jigsaw WA, 2000, is an excellent history of this organisation. This quote is from p.108.

68 Meggitt describes the process of speaking truth to power in her thesis, 'The Role of Self Help in the Development of Public Policy'.

69 The new shape of the Australian family was revealed by the Institute for Family Studies' *Australian Family Formation Project, 1981–82*. Papers stressing grief and suffering were given to the Third Australian Conference on Adoption by Kate Inglis, Margaret Van Keppel and Robin Winkler, see Oxenbury (ed), *Changing Families*. Judith McHutchinson's 'Statement on Behalf of Relinquishing Mothers and Their Friends' was made to the same conference and circulated widely through the adoption community.

These women were 'delighted to have come together, and to have found so much in common, so much to share'.

> They are going back to their home states armed with the knowledge that they are not alone anymore. Even those who cannot now acknowledge their relinquishment in public can draw strength from the support of others... They... are now determined to put an end to the conspiracy of silence surrounding adoption, and to make the community aware that the relinquishment of a child is the most heartbreakingly painful thing a woman can do.

Prior to the conference the language of pain and suffering was not much used in reform circles. Jigsaw activists were more inclined to follow the CSMC social justice model, speaking in terms of a civic right to access information. ARMS was to validate the public confession of suffering, for mothers and in time for adoptees as well.[70]

Women returning from the conference founded branches of ARMS in their capital cities. In Victoria Marie Meggitt worked with Western Australian researchers Margaret Van Keppel and Robin Winkler to distribute a national questionnaire to ARMS members asking them to detail their experience of relinquishing their babies. Again the impact was to confirm a shared sense of loss and deprivation. At the inaugural meeting of ARMS Western Australia in October 1982 the speaker presented the political movement towards secrecy and sealed records as a push by adopting parents to completely own the children they adopted. She concluded with a civic call to arms:

> Natural mothers have never been consulted as to what they would like to see go into the Adoption 'Agreement'. In 86 years of adoption practice your point of view has never been presented to the law-makers. As an organised body, you can have a voice, for the very first time.

A year later an article in the Western Australian *Daily Mail* put the ARMS case in more psychologised terms:

> The mothers are determined to explode the myth that the natural mother wants secrecy, that after their child is adopted they 'go away

---

70   Robert Bender's paper to the Second Australian Conference on Adoption, 'Rights of Adopted Persons', followed the CSMC social justice model; see Picton (ed.), *Current Concerns and Alternatives*.

and forget', and that the birth of subsequent children wipes out the grief and anguish of the loss of an earlier child by adoption.

By 1985 Jigsaw WA had taken up the language of suffering, urging members to speak up at public meetings: 'It is only as we truthfully let our suffering be known, that injustice will be supplanted by laws which do not hurt'.[71]

In South Australia, two members of the Council of Single Mothers and their Children organised a Mothers' Day phone-in in May 1983 for mothers separated from their children by adoption. The three hundred women who responded became the founding members of ARMS SA. Meeting in self-help groups, they learned that experience shared could become experience understood. Members soon moved into political action, working to open the sealed birth records alongside Jigsaw SA and a small supportive group of adoptive parents. In 1988 Meg Hale attended an adoption conference in Melbourne with the chairperson of ARMS SA and they took the opportunity to discuss their South Australian campaign with the Victorian activists. Members of ARMS Victoria warned them against asking for too much in the first round of legislation. 'Fight for the adoptees now and come back and argue for birth mothers in a few years' time. If you ask for it all now, you'll end up with nothing!' But as they drove back to Adelaide, Valma and Meg decided that in all justice they could only support legislation which opened the records to mothers as well as adoptees. And in 1988 they won that from the South Australian legislature—the first in the English speaking world to give mothers separated by adoption the right to apply for identifying information about their children. The South Australian Act also contained provisions for 'Open Adoption', allowing birth parents and adopting parents to register agreements establishing ground rules for the exchange of information and continuing contact between child and birth parents—a great advance on the 'conditional consents' of the Victorian Act.[72]

Across the next decade, campaigns in the other states achieved similar reforms. None was more generous in its provisions than the South Australian Act. South Australian activists credit their success to a reformist Labor government, sympathetic politicians in all parties (some with personal ex-

---

71 Jan Kashin provided the research team with a copy of Marie Meggitt's letter to the ARMS network distributing the Van Keppel questionnaire. The WA opening address has been published by Shirley Moulds as Submission 213a to the Senate inquiry into forced adoption (see note 9 above). Elphick cites the *Daily Mail* article and exhortation to members. *The Adoption Jigsaw*, 90 and 117.

72 Meg Hale told Marian Quartly her story in a telephone interview in September 2012. The South Australian Adoption Act 1988 can be accessed at http://my.lawlex.com.au/

SPEAKING TRUTH TO POWER

perience of adoption), and a moderate, non-militant approach from ARMS SA. ARMS members also established a close relationship with the adoption office in the state department for community welfare. After the records were opened, the department regularly referred their adoption clients to ARMS for assistance with searching and making contact, and all forms of counselling relating to adoption. In 1989 ARMS SA won ongoing funding to employ a co-ordinator/social worker: the only support group run entirely by mothers to receive government funding in Australia.

A similar transition took place in Victoria, where Jigsaw, ARMS and the Adoptive Families Association of Victoria came together in 1988 to establish a single government-funded agency, the Victorian Adoption Network for Information and Self-Help. VANISH took on the full range of funded adoption related services, including advice to intending adoptive parents. Jigsaw Victoria took itself out of existence, and ARMS Victoria and AFAV returned to their origins as nonprofessional mutual help groups.[73]

That the old reform groups could work so readily with adoption professionals is evidence of changing attitudes on both sides of the equation, but mostly on the professional side. By the mid-eighties new recruits to social work were educated in universities where many of their lecturers were feminists, sceptical about power relations in the family, and ready to see single mothers as victims of patriarchy. Psychology was a required subject in social work degrees, and students learnt to understand family relationships in psychologised terms; to read, for example, an adopted teenager's rejection of his adopted family in terms of 'genealogical bewilderment'—'the absence of knowledge of past origins and concern about a family identity'. Graduates encountered 'tea room talk' about undocumented, irregular practices in the 'bad' old days of pre-reform adoption, and looked to the new forms of open adoption as truly 'in the best interest of the child'.[74]

By 1993 the social work profession was committed to a form of adoption which explicitly rejected the practices of the 1960s. On the advice of their social work administrators the Commonwealth Council of Social Welfare

---

73   The adoption acts were as follows: Tasmania 1988; New South Wales 1990 and 2000; ACT 1993; Western Australia 1994; Northern Territory 1994; Queensland 2009. For the Victorian situation see 'History of Vanish', Vanish website, http://www.vanish.org.au/

74   For changing attitudes amongst academic social workers see articles by Bill Healy, 'Elements in the Development of an Australian Radical Social Work' and Elaine Martin and Judith Healy, 'Social Work as Women's Work: Census Data 1976–1986'. *Australian Social Work* 46(1) (1993): 3–8; and 46(4): 13–18. Christine Vickers reflected on changes in adoption and social work practice in her contribution to Ceridwen Spark and Denise Cuthbert (eds), *Other People's Children: Adoption in Australia*. North Melbourne: Australian Scholarly Publishing (2009): 95–109.

Ministers endorsed a set of 'National Minimum Principles in Adoption'. These included the propositions that while adoption was valuable for some children:

> Adoption is a service for children, not for adults wishing to acquire the care of a child; [and]

> A child has the right to be brought up within their birth family, wherever possible.

The ministers also confirmed that adult adoptees and birth parents had a right to identifying information about each other, though vetos could be placed on contact by either party. And they endorsed open adoption,

> where ongoing contact between the birth parents and their child occurs following adoption proceedings and is acknowledged in the adoption order.

This position pitted the profession directly against groups of adoptive parents, particularly in Western Australia and Queensland, where their lobbying blocked and temporally undid legal reforms.[75]

Social workers might have hoped for an alliance with adoptees and birth parents. A leading social work administrator described the virtues of the new adoption to the 1994 Australian Adoption Conference, and candidly admitted the faults of the old: 'By *present* feminist standards it may be said that we colluded in maintaining a system of secrecy and shame'. She called on the conference to 'move beyond blaming and mutual recrimination'. But this was not to be.[76]

ORIGINS AND FORCED SEPARATION

With the opening of the previously sealed birth records, the agitation by mothers and adoptees moved into a new phase. Groups which did not receive government funding for their search and counselling facilities struggled to survive. Their memberships were 'continually revolving'; in the words of the president of Jigsaw WA 'As each desired relative is found, members drop

---

75   The document 'National Minimum Principles in Adoption' was included as Appendix 2 in the Western Australian 'Adoption Legislative Review: Adoptions Act (1994): Final Report', 1997. Elphick describes the anti-reform movements on p.220 of *The Adoption Jigsaw*.

76   Margaret MacDonald, at the 1994 Australian Adoption Conference. See *Has Adoption a Future?*, 16.

away'. Long-term members were often those whose relatives could not be found, and those whose meetings with lost relatives had not satisfied their sense of absence and incompleteness.[77]

For some mothers separated by adoption the open records exacerbated their sense of loss and moved them into a new kind of action. Dian Wellfare lost her child to adoption in 1968. In 2005 she would be one of the founders of Origins NSW, a group dedicated to the task of righting the wrongs of women who were, in the language of Origins, forcibly separated from their children by adoption. Wellfare dated the beginning of her campaign to 'the moment I was given a copy of my social work records... in 1991'. Those files included a comment from the social worker managing her case.

> She [Wellfare] expressed she wanted to keep the baby very strongly confident in her pregnancy and is elated by it. Knows her mother would not turn her away from home with the baby.

Wellfare had no memory of this confidence, this elation. She knew that she needed to discover what had changed her mind: 'why I would have left him in the hospital if I had intended to keep him?'[78]

Wellfare learnt from Judy McHutchison, the founder of ARMS NSW, that the focus of agitation should include the 'illicit adoption practices' used against mothers; 'the law was the only weapon we had to force people to listen to us'. McHutchison was a professional researcher who had gathered a large body of material about the history of adoption in Australia. McHutchison and Wellfare were assisted by the Public Advocacy Interest Centre to mount cases for damages against the State of New South Wales. Kim Taylor in Queensland also took the State to court. All these cases were eventually lost, through difficulties with statutes limiting the time frame within which evidence could be brought forward.[79]

Chris Cole was also moved to action by the evidence of illicit practices revealed in her medical records. In 1994 Cole and Wellfare presented papers to the 1994 Australian Adoption Conference 'exposing adoption fraud'. Cole demonstrated in documented detail that:

---

77   Elphick describes the loss of enthusiasm, *The Adoption Jigsaw*, 64.
78   Origins Inc New South Wales, 'Our History, Australia'. http://www.originsnsw.com/ When Wellfare died in April 2008, Origins established a site, *Dian Wellfare: Adoption Rights Campaigner*, where one can access Wellfare's autobiographical fragments.
79   Information in this paragraph comes from Jennie Burrows and Chris Cole. For McHutchison and Wellfare's legal cases see the report of the Public Interest Advocacy Centre in *Releasing the Past: Adoption Practices 1950–1998: Final Report*. NSW Parliamentary Paper number 6000, Standing Committee on Social Issues, 8 December 2000, 175.

My medical records revealed... that I had signed the consent form for my daughter's adoption, not only under duress, but also under the effects of a strong hypnotic barbiturate... Before I signed the consent form I was still the guardian of my child and had every right to see, hold and feed her, before being given the hormone tablets to dry up my milk... I was, to put it very bluntly and honestly, coerced into giving my baby up.[80]

A social work educator from England was moved by their 'burning sense of injustice' to read a statement to the last session of the conference.

As a social worker I listen to the rage and grief and despair of birthparents and I cannot say that I am o.k., I personally didn't do this... I want to say, now, to the birthparents here that I am desperately saddened by, and sorry for, the things that I as a social worker have done, as a member of that profession, to them... I believe that all professionals in adoption need to acknowledge their personal and collective responsibility, that they are interwoven and inseparable, because that is what it means to be a profession.

At the next adoption conference in 1997 the New South Wales branch of the Australian Association of Social Workers issued a statement expressing 'extreme regret at the lifelong pain experienced by many women who have relinquished their children for adoption'.[81]

Cole, Wellfare and ten other women founded Origins NSW in April 1995. In the words of their website, the founders wanted to bring to public attention 'the severe emotional anguish, trauma, and grief left in the wake of their adoption experience'. From the first they made 'illicit adoption practices the focal point of our organisation'. State branches of Origins were formed in Queensland and then Tasmania and Victoria, and all over the country researchers began collecting historical information about adoption.[82]

---

80 The papers by Chris Cole and Dian Wellfare, both called 'Exposing Adoption Fraud', may be found in McDonald (ed), *Has Adoption a Future?*

81 Murray Ryburn, Social Worker and Lecturer, University of Birmingham UK. His statement was not printed in the conference proceedings, but copies have long circulated amongst the adoption community. The AASW NSW apology is cited in *Releasing the Past*, 183: para 10.108.

82 Origins Inc New South Wales, 'Our History, Australia', http://www.originsnsw.com/. The quote from Cole is from an email communication dated May 2013 in the possession of the authors.

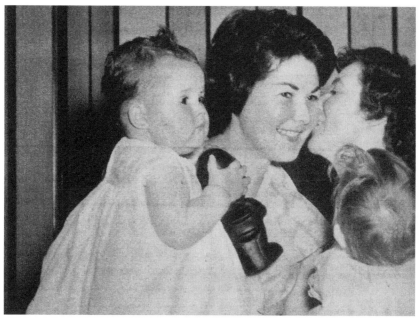

4.1 This mother and her adopted baby daughter won the national Australian Women's Weekly 'Happy Mother and Baby' contest in October 1963. The prize 'aimed at finding an obviously healthy and happy mother and child with a well-adjusted relationship'. *Australian Women's Weekly*, 16 October 1963, p.7.

With permission *Australian Women's Weekly.*

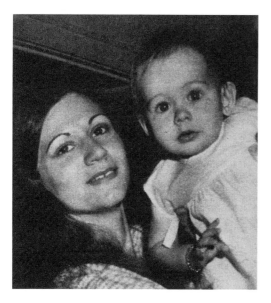

4.2 The *Australian Women's Weekly* reported in April 1972 the story of 'Elizabeth', a single mother, who had decided to bring up her baby on her own. It was an entirely positive report. *Australian Women's Weekly*, 5 April 1972, p.6.

With permission *Australian Women's Weekly.*

4.3 Aboriginal and White anti-adoption lobby groups joined to lead the International Women's Day March, Brisbane, 1994. Janice Benson (Jan Kashin) is standing in the centre under the banner.

Photograph courtesy Jan Kashin

4.4 Christine Cole and Ristin Nichols leading the Women's Day March in Sydney, 11 March 1995.

Sunday Telegraph, 12 March 1995, p.3. Photograph by Nick Cubbin.
With permission Newspix (for *Sunday Telegraph*)

4.5 'Nuns sorry for forced adoption.' *West Australian*, 7 April 2010, p.15.
Judith Hendriksen won an apology from the Perth Sisters of Mercy for their part in her
separation from her daughter Anne.
© Albany Advertiser/West Australian Newspapers, with permission.

In mid-1996 a Tasmanian newspaper reported that 50 mothers in that
state had been told that their babies had died, only to be found by those same
babies when the adoption records were opened. Origins NSW fanned the
flames, generating a front-page article headed 'BABYSNATCHERS' in the
Sydney Morning Herald. The story was taken up by other newspapers, state
and national, and by radio and TV. Origins members told their stories in
media interviews, especially talk-back radio. In Tasmania the publicity led
the Minister for Community and Health Services to commission a report
'on issues relating to historical adoption practices' in that state. The report
was unable to point to specific cases of 'babysnatching', but did suggest the
need for legal reforms. Members of Origins and Jigsaw Tasmania seized
this opportunity to lobby their local members, generating questions in
parliament and pushing for a more comprehensive inquiry. One speaker told
the Tasmanian Legislative Council that he was moved by the pain of his
electors; 'they are continuing to suffer as a result of... having their children
removed', and an inquiry might have a 'healing, soothing effect'. In 1999 a
select committee of both houses of parliament was set up to inquire into 'the
past and continuing effects of professional practices in the administration

and delivery of adoption and related services', and whether these practices were unethical or unlawful.[83]

In New South Wales Origins developed a technique of lobbying local members, asking them to present a statement of Origins' grievances to parliament. It was so successful that four such statements were tabled in two weeks in November 1997. Rallies attracted media attention, and members 'bared their souls' in 'emotive' interviews on ABC and commercial television. Wellfare remembered that

> many more either found the courage to attend the public rally or expose their identities through the media. As traumatic as it was, everyone did their bit. We were not going to hide in shame any longer.

The Labor MP Pat Ryan was Chris Cole's local representative, and she persuaded him to take up the cause. His lobbying brought more politicians onside, and in 1998 a new Minister for Community Services announced a parliamentary inquiry into 'the professional practices in the administration and delivery of adoption and related services' and any 'unethical and unlawful practices' that this might have involved.[84]

Both of these inquiries provided a public platform for mothers and adoptees to tell their stories of pain and suffering. The Tasmanian committee reported that they were moved by the courage of the witnesses, but could not 'make any definitive finding' about unethical or unlawful practices. The New South Wales report was much more thoroughly researched, thanks in part to the work of Origins, and much more comprehensive in what it covered. Its introduction acknowledged that

> many mothers who gave up their children to adoption were denied their rights, and did not uncaringly give away their children.

It recommended that

> The New South Wales Government should issue a statement of public acknowledgement that past adoption practices were misguided, and that, on occasions unethical and unlawful practices have occurred

---

83   Ann Cunningham, 'Background Paper for the Minister of Community and Health Services on Issues Relating to Historical Adoption in Tasmania', 4 December 1996. For the statements by politicians see *Hansard* for the Tasmanian Lower House and Legislative Council, 2 October 1997 and 22 April 1999.

84   The story is told in 'Just How Did the Inquiry Get Got?' www.originsnsw.com/ nswinquiry2/.

causing lasting suffering for many mothers, fathers, adoptees and their families.

It did not promise any legal redress for this suffering, but did recommend a review of the Limitation Act.[85]

Origins, Jigsaw and ARMS groups in other states pushed hard for similar inquiries. Conservative governments were unmoved, preferring the advice of pro-adoption parents' groups. Labor opposition members were more sympathetic. In Victoria the shadow community services minister Christine Campbell told parliament in 1997 that the coercion practised on single mothers demanded an inquiry, and Labor made that an election promise in 1999. But once elected, the Bracks government reneged on that promise. A government spokesperson said that 'the broader community' in the area of adoption did not support the inquiry, but documents obtained by Origins Victoria suggested that the government feared that the inquiry would produce 'substantial criticism of hospitals, medical staff, social workers, religious organisations and welfare agencies', together with 'claims for compensation'.[86]

A NATIONAL APOLOGY FOR THE PAIN OF FORCED ADOPTION

This public performance of the pain and suffering of adoption took place in a wider context of public grief and government response. In the decade 1995–2005 three national enquiries into the treatment of children in state care revealed suffering, neglect and mistreatment on a massive scale. Though these were national inquiries, the practices they condemned were all administered by State governments under State law. The inquiry of the Human Rights and Equal Opportunity Commission into the removal of Aboriginal children reported in 1997 that between one in three and one in ten of all Indigenous children were forcibly removed from their families and communities in the years between 1910 and 1970, inflicting huge psychological damage—the 'Stolen Generations'. The Commonwealth Senate Community Affairs References Committee report on the migration of

---

85   The Tasmanian report was published as 'Parliament of Tasmania. Joint Select Committee. Adoption and Related Services, 1950–1988'. Hobart, Tasmania, 1999. The quotations here from the NSW report *Releasing the Past*, are from recommendations 15 and 16.

86   The Victorian case is described in two articles in *The Age*: 'The Pain of a Mother Deprived', 28 May 2005; and Jewel Topside, 'Adoption Files Opened to Mothers', 7 August, 2004. Origins Victoria had to take their case to the Victorian Civil and Administrative Tribunal to get the documents released.

British and Maltese children to Australia—'The Lost Innocents: Righting the Record'—revealed in 2001 that over six decades many thousands of children had been brought to Australia, often to be brutally mistreated in institutions 'where abuse and assault… was a daily occurrence and where hardship, hard work and indifferent care was the norm'. In 2004 the same Senate committee reported on the treatment of the 'Forgotten Australians'— the 500,000 or more Australians who experienced institutional care last century—finding widespread abuse, neglect and humiliation, and an almost total absence of love, affection and nurturing.

All these inquiries drew heavily on evidence from those who had suffered, and all commended the bravery of those who spoke publicly of their suffering. The Stolen Generations report opened with the words:

> Grief and loss are the predominant themes of this report… Much of its subject matter is so personal and intimate that ordinarily it would not be discussed. These matters have only been discussed with the Inquiry with great difficulty and much personal distress. The suffering and the courage of those who have told their stories inspire sensitivity and respect.

All the reports recommended that such suffering required a formal apology; 'the first step in any compensation and healing for victims of gross violations of human rights must be an acknowledgement of the truth and the delivery of an apology'. The two Senate Inquiries called on the Commonwealth Government to issue a formal statement acknowledging the nation's part in the suffering.[87]

---

87   The reports are: HREOC's *Bringing Them Home*, 1997, at
      www.hreoc.gov.au/pdf/social_justice/bringing_them_home_report.pdf;
      the Senate Community Affairs References Committee, *Lost Innocents*, 2001, at
      http://www.aph.gov.au/Parliamentary_Business/Committees/Senate_
      Committees?url=clac_ctte/completed_inquiries/1999-02/child_migrat/index.htm;
      the Senate Community Affairs References Committee, *Forgotten Australians*,
      2004, at http://www.aph.gov.au/Parliamentary_Business/Committees/Senate_
      Committees?url=clac_ctte/completed_inquiries/2004-07/inst_care/index.htm.

      See also the Senate Community Affairs References Committee's inquiry into the
      implementation of the two previous reports, at
      http://www.aph.gov.au/Parliamentary_Business/Committees/Senate_
      Committees?url=clac_ctte/completed_inquiries/2008-10/recs_lost_innocents_
      forgotten_aust_rpts/index.htm

      The quotations here are from *Lost Innocents* recommendations 14 and 30; and
      Forgotten Australians recommendation 1. The Report of the Senate Community
      Affairs References Committee into *Commonwealth contribution to former forced
      adoption policies and practices*, February 2012, is to be found at

The Rudd Labor government responded with two national apologies: in 2008 to the Stolen Generations 'for the removal of Aboriginal and Torres Strait Islander children from their families, their communities and their country'; and in 2009 both to the child migrants and to all children institutionalised over the previous century—an apology 'for all these injustices to you, as children, who were placed in our care'.

Mothers and children separated by adoption argued that their experience was very much the same as that suffered by Aboriginal families and institutionalised children, and pressed hard for this to be recognised by government. They were initially led to believe that they would be included in the second apology in 2009, and their omission caused sorrow and anger amongst the members of ARMS, Origins, and those who were beginning to call themselves the Mothers of the Stolen White Generations.[88]

Christine Cole had set up her Apology Alliance in February 2008, in response to the national apology to the Stolen Generations. Cole formally launched a campaign to achieve state and national apologies to mothers and children separated by adoption. Success came first locally. In Queensland the group ALAS, Adoption.Loss.Adult.Support, received an apology from the Royal Brisbane and Women's Hospital in June 2009, and in September the Anglican Archbishop of Queensland said sorry on behalf of a mother's home in Toowong. In Perth in April 2010 the Sisters of Mercy asked forgiveness for forced adoption in a private hospital under their control. These and other local apologies were cited in debates in the Western Australian parliament which resulted in an apology by the state premier, supported by the opposition, to 'the mothers, their children and families who were adversely affected by... adoption practices'.[89]

---

http://www.aph.gov.au/Parliamentary_Business/Committees/Senate_Committees?url=clac_ctte/completed_inquiries/2010-13/comm_contrib_former_forced_adoption/index.htm

88 For Prime Minister Kevin Rudd's apology to the Stolen Generations see http://australia.gov.au/about-australia/our-country/our-people/apology-to-australias-indigenous-peoples. For Prime Minister Kevin Rudd's apology to the Forgotten Australians and former child migrants, see http://pandora.nla.gov.au/pan/110625/20091116-1801/www.pm.gov.au/node/6321.html

The national apologies are discussed in Denise Cuthbert and Marian Quartly '"Forced Adoption" in the Australian Story of National Regret and Apology'. *Australian Journal of Politics and History* 58 (2012): 82–96; and Cuthbert and Quartly, 'Forced Child Removal and the Politics of National Apologies in Australia'. *American Indian Quarterly* 37(1–2) (Winter-Spring 2013): 178–202. For mothers of the Stolen White Generations see http://whitestolengeneration.com/

89 For the ALAS-gained apology see Submission 226 to the Senate inquiry into forced adoption (see note 42 above). The letter from the Anglican Archbishop Dr Phillip

At Federal level Rachel Siewert, the chair of the Senate Community Affairs References Committee, moved in June 2010 that the Senate

> recognises the grief, pain and anguish suffered by thousands of mothers who were victims of the forced adoption policies implemented by state governments for decades; and acknowledges: (i) this pain and grief is on-going, and (ii) these mothers deserve an apology for the pain and anguish they have suffered and continue to suffer.

The motion was lost on the vote. Siewert did not give up; in November 2010 she asked the Senate to authorise an inquiry into the role of the Commonwealth Government, its policies and practices, in contributing to forced adoptions. This time she could point to the recent apology of the Western Australian parliament, and this time the motion was passed.[90]

The Senate inquiry reported in February 2012. It called for a national apology formally acknowledging 'the harm suffered by many parents whose children were forcibly removed and by the children who were separated from their parents'. It also called for similar apologies from state and territory governments, and from institutions administering adoption. As this book goes to print, all state parliaments have made their apologies, together with all of the major religious and government institutions involved in adoption. The Australian Association of Social Workers has issued a statement acknowledging the realities of forced adoption and admitting the involvement of some social workers, though this position remains controversial within the profession.[91]

On 21 March 2013 the Australian federal parliament, 'on behalf of the Australian people, [took] responsibility and [apologised] for the policies and practices that forced the separation of mothers from their babies, which created a lifelong legacy of pain and suffering'. In delivering the apology

---

Aspinall, 23 September, 2009, has been circulated on the internet. The apology from the Perth Sisters of Mercy was reported in Daniel Emerson, 'Nuns Say Sorry for Forced adoption'. *West Australian*, 7 April, 2010, 15. The apology from the Western Australian Premier, David Barnett, is to be found in the *Western Australian Parliamentary Debates*, Assembly, 19 October 2010.

90   See Senator Rachel Siewert, 'Motion: Adoption'. *Commonwealth Parliamentary Debates (CPD)*, Senate, 15 June 2010, 3250–3251; and 'Motion: Community Affairs References Committee'. *CPD*, Senate, 1 November 2010, 1173.

91   For the report of the Senate inquiry into forced adoption, see note 87 above. The Australian Association of Social Workers' apology is to be found in 'Acknowledgement: Acknowledging birth mothers who experienced being forced to relinquish their child'. *AASW National Bulletin, Newsletter of the Australian Association of Social Workers Ltd* 22(3) (Winter 2012):27.

the Prime Minister, Julia Gillard, spoke of its national significance, as 'a profound act of moral insight by a nation searching its conscience... to right an old wrong and to face a hard truth'. It took a lot of courage for a nation to look into its past and recognise its mistakes, but 'this is part of the process of a nation growing up'. The story of adoption, she said, was

> A story of suffering and unbearable loss.
>
> But ultimately a story of strength, as those affected by forced adoptions found their voice.
>
> Organised and shared their experiences.
>
> And, by speaking truth to power, brought about the Apology we offer today.[92]

---

92 For Julia Gillard's apology to those affected by forced adoption practices, see http://www.pm.gov.au/press-office/national-apology-forced-adoptions

CHAPTER 5

THE RISE AND FALL OF
INTERCOUNTRY ADOPTION

The Commonwealth apology to those separated by forced adoption did not include those affected by intercountry adoption. This exclusion was made despite representations from activists and academics urging the inclusion of adoptees from overseas. The government's focus on domestic adoption allowed it to locate the practice of exploitation firmly in the past, never to happen again. Thus it could ignore the current realities of intercountry adoption and, most recently, surrogacy.

We argue here that the stories of domestic and intercountry adoption have run together in Australia. The market forces driving domestic adoption have also driven intercountry adoption, producing the same relationships of power and inequality between those adopting babies and those giving them up. The administration of intercountry adoption within Australia has been managed by the same State Government welfare departments that administer domestic adoption, though the Commonwealth Department of Foreign Affairs has been involved because of Australia's endorsement of international conventions governing the exchange of children between nations. The major difference between local and intercountry adoption is that while the local variety has been reformed to make it open and inclusive of all the families involved, distance, poverty and poor record keeping in the sending countries has often made this kind of inclusion impossible.

The story of intercountry adoption has its own rhythm and its own logic, and it makes sense to tell it in a separate chapter. But the context of local adoption is always present and active.

Intercountry adoption first hit the Australian headlines in 1972: 'War babies smuggled in by air'; '"Mothers" to fight for Vietnam babies'. When Melbourne secretary Elaine Moir landed at Sydney Airport on 29 May with five Vietnamese children whom she proposed to 'smuggle' into Australia, she created a political and media storm. Acting in defiance of State and

Commonwealth authorities, Moir already had five Australian families lined up to adopt the 'waifs', who were aged between 16 months and three and a half years. The children had been granted exit visas from Vietnam but had been refused entry permits for Australia. 'I had no trouble getting them aboard the jet', said Ms Moir, 'BOAC gave me every co-operation'. Although no formal adoption procedures had been completed in Australia the children were speedily handed over to their eager new parents. Mrs Colin Stewart, whose child Nuyen had reportedly been found abandoned on a Saigon rubbish heap, was adamant: 'I've got my little baby and that's all that matters'. The Stewarts had tried about twelve times to adopt an Australian child but were 'refused all down the line'. So they decided to take matters into their own hands. 'The chance of having a Vietnamese child came up and we grabbed at it'. The Saigon courts had approved the proxy adoptions so the Stewarts saw no reason to 'go through all the legal rigmarole' again in Australia. 'If the Australian authorities try to take my baby away from me now, I think I'll kill myself', said Mrs Stewart. 'They wouldn't dare, would they?' Another adopting mother, Miss Cecilia Verlinden from Ballarat, was equally defiant. 'I won't give her back' she said of her 3-year-old daughter. 'I'll fight to the last to keep her... to get her they'll have to kidnap her'.[93]

While State authorities legally controlled adoption, the Federal government was in charge of immigration. Both struggled to manage the vexed issue of adopting overseas sourced 'orphans'. When confronted with Elaine Moir's fait accompli, both State and Federal bureaus were compelled to act. While they allowed the children to stay with their new parents, they did require them to go through local adoption procedures.

Elaine Moir's defiant rescue mission and the strident voices of the adopting parents set the stage for the power struggle that shaped intercountry adoption in Australia in the last decades of the twentieth century. The major players in this tug-of-war were State and Federal authorities, Church representatives and pro-adoption parent lobby groups. Although Moir's babies were not the first to be adopted from overseas, her mission and the children she rescued captured the public's imagination. Public expectations were raised about the abundance of available orphans and the ease with which they could be harvested from orphanages in war-torn, poverty-stricken countries.

---

93   Quotations in these first paragraphs are from 'War Babies Smuggled in by Air'. *Canberra Times,* 29 May 1972, 1 (NAA A1838, 3014/10/15/6 PART I, 227–228) and '"Mothers" to Fight for Vietnam Babies'. *Sydney Morning Herald,* 29 May 1972, 3.

RESCUING THE VICTIMS OF WAR

Australians have long proposed adoption as a patriotic response to crises overseas. When Australia was drawn into the First World War, novelist Ethel Turner wrote in the *Sydney Morning Herald* on 23 September 1914 that 'any Australian mother who can do so should take a war orphan into her heart and home'. The call to adopt war orphans was a sentiment voiced throughout the 'war to end all wars'. The following month Turner proposed a large scale program for intercountry adoption, including a four step plan for adopting 'a child in distress'. 'I say with absolute confidence', she wrote

> that if next Monday 5000 British and Belgian and French children arrived, wistful-eyed and bewildered, at Circular Quay, by Friday every one of them would be eagerly absorbed and made welcome in Australian homes.[94]

Plans to adopt overseas orphans were mostly thwarted by distance and logistics, though Henri Tovel was one exception. Tovel, a French orphan, became the mascot of an Australian squadron during the British occupation of France in 1919, and was successfully smuggled into Australia and adopted by one of his soldier sponsors (see Fig. 5.1). In the interwar period there were attempts to bring orphaned babies from Britain to Australia as part of a child migration scheme, but with a surplus of homegrown babies available, schemes for 'overseas adoption' were not widely supported.[95]

As we have already discussed, by the time Australia entered the Second World War, demand for babies was rising. Calls made in parliament for 'Australians to bring relief to Britain by offering homes to… child refugees' quickly translated in the media into a proposal for large-scale intercountry adoption. An article in the *Australian Woman's Weekly* in December 1941 entitled 'Adoptions help cure war heartaches' proclaimed that 'the next best thing when you can't have a baby yourself is to adopt some motherless scrap of humanity you can love'. The leaders of the Australian National Council of Women played the patriotic theme:

---

94   Ethel Turner, 'Wartime VIII: The Cry of Children', and 'War Orphans'. *Sydney Morning Herald*, 23 September 1914, 12, and 14 October 1914, 10.

95   Henri Tovel's 'interesting history' attracted much attention in Australian newspapers, especially after he was killed in a motor car accident in 1928. See, for example, 'Air Force "Mascot". French War Orphan. Accidental Death in Melbourne'. *Western Argus* (Kalgoorlie), 29 May 1928, 28. For the child migration scheme see Joshua Forkert, *Orphans of Vietnam: A History of Intercountry Adoption Policy and Practice in Australia, 1968–75*. PhD thesis, University of Adelaide, 2012: 59–60.

The Board feels that here lies opportunity for Australian women to give definite and valuable assistance to the Empire at this critical moment by opening their homes and their hearts to little children from overseas.

Members responded enthusiastically: 'we have no doubt that many people who would not otherwise thought of adopting children will be only too glad to open their homes and hearts to little victims of war'.[96] Thousands of couples registered their interest in adopting a child from Britain, but the child migrant scheme that eventuated did not involve adoption.

In her letter to the *Argus* in March 1947, Helen P. Meggs of Hawthorn proposed the obvious solution to the shortage of locally available babies; to satisfy demand by importing from overseas:

For some years past the demand in Australia for babies for adoption has been far greater than the supply. At the same time, politicians have been tearing their thinning hair over the threatened decline in the population. Also, for some years past, babies have been dying like flies all over the rest of the world—chiefly from starvation. In the case of any commercial article we import what we cannot produce locally until the demand is satisfied. Why not do the same with babies?

The large-scale dislocations of people that followed the end of the European war suggested a possible source. Margaret Watts, a humanitarian who had worked for decades rescuing children displaced by war, reported from England in 1949 that

[while] there were no British or Allied children available... she felt that... something [should] be done about German orphans under 7 years of age.

A few displaced children from Germany and Greece were brought to Australia in these years, but the numbers were very small. Adoption advocates began to look further afield.[97]

---

96 The *Australian Women's Weekly* promoted war adoption in an article 'Adoptions Help Cure War Heartaches. Foundlings and orphans are more in demand than ever', 13 December 1941, 10. The Australian National Council of Women discussed adoption at meetings of the NSW Board, 6 June 1940, minutes held in the Mitchell Library MLMSS3739 MLK 03011, and of the national Board, minutes held in the National Library of Australia, 7 August 1940, Box 12, MS7583 NLA.

97 Helen P. Meggs, 'Import Babies'. Letter to the Editor. *Argus*, 29 March 1947, 18. Minutes of the Meeting of the Australian National Council of Women of NSW

In the US, the Korean War triggered a huge increase in intercountry adoption. Interest in Australia was also aroused by the prospect of homeless babies, but Australian governments were reluctant to assist intending parents to adopt overseas. Graeme Gregory, a minister and social worker involved for many years with Methodist child care services, blamed this reluctance on 'Australian racism'. He recalled that in the 1950s and 60s practices under the White Australia Policy inhibited the adoption into Australia of 'child victims of the Korean conflict'. Even members of the Australian occupation forces who fathered children in Japan had difficulties in adopting these children or bringing them to Australia. A further problem lay with the social workers who increasingly controlled the process of domestic adoption across the 1950s and 1960s. Australians who adopted children whilst living overseas reported years of delay in getting their adoptions approved by the Australian authorities.[98]

By the end of the 1960s the winds of change blew the issue of intercountry adoption to the surface again. The Vietnam War created the perfect storm. Immigration policy was slowly changing, as were attitudes to race, humanitarianism and political activism. 1972 was a watershed year in raising people's hopes. Australia had been under conservative rule for twenty-three years and the Federal ALP was riding a wave of renewed optimism, one that would take them to electoral victory that year. Australia was deeply embedded in the quagmire of the conflict in Vietnam, an unpopular war seen by many as a political and strategic failure. Opponents and supporters of the war were united in a collective sense of guilt by reports of its toll on the civilian population of Vietnam, and especially on the children. Some opportunity for public redemption was seen to lie with the tens of thousands of children said to be orphaned by the war. When Rev Denis Oakley returned from a World Vision tour of South Vietnam in October 1972 he reported that there were '126 registered orphanages catering for about 20,000 orphans in South Vietnam'. 'We've helped create this problem', he proclaimed, 'let's do something to help repair it'.[99]

Executive, 30 June 1949.

98 Graeme Gregory, 'Intercountry Adoption—An Agency View'. In Picton (ed.), *Proceedings of the First Australian Conference on Adoption*, 41. For the 'Diggers' waifs' left in Japan and the racism exhibited over their possible migration to Australia, see Catriona Elder's article '"Diggers' Waifs": Desire, Anxiety and Immigration in Post-1945 Australia'. *Australian Historical Studies*, 38 (issue 130) (2007): 261–278.

99 'Help These Vietnamese Orphans, Says Cleric'. *The Age*, 16 October 1972. NAA A1838, 3014/10/15/6 PART I, 168.

Harrowing stories of the appalling conditions in Vietnamese orphanages heightened humanitarian concerns. 'Death Faces Vietnam Waifs', read a headline in the *Sydney Morning Herald* in June 1972. Mrs Celia Barclay, an English Quaker working on Vietnamese orphanage projects, told readers that nine hundred of every one thousand Vietnamese war orphans in average orphanages would be dead before they were one year old. Epidemics, infections, pneumonia, dehydration and diarrhoea took their toll of children in the first year of their life. By the time the survivors were sixteen or seventeen and left the orphanages, it was only a hope that twenty-five of the original thousand would be alive. A largely sympathetic media supported pro-adoption parent groups, church agencies and a number of politicians on both sides of the political divide who argued for the only solution thought possible at the time, the evacuation of orphans out of war-ravaged Saigon to the arms of loving parents in the safety of Australian homes. Elaine Moir's mission and others like it were seen as nothing short of heroic.[100]

By January 1973 the Australian Adoptive Families Association (AAFA) had been formed. Rosemary Calder, mother of an adopted Vietnamese child, became their chief advocate. Calder later described the 'groundswell of emotion' surrounding the Indo Chinese War as the result of 'media coverage' of 'the plight of civilians in a war—women and children'. Television brought the Vietnam War into the living rooms of ordinary people around the world and 'Australian families... responded... by offering themselves as families to the children left orphaned by that war'. Calder provided Rena Briand (Huxley) with the names of AAFA members ready, willing and able to adopt children from overseas, and Briand and others defied the authorities, undertaking what they saw as rescue missions to Saigon to bring children back to Australia.[101]

On 24 October 1973 a cable sent from the Australian embassy in Saigon to Canberra authorities warned the Australian government that Mrs R.E. Huxley had arrived in Saigon a few days earlier armed with a letter stating that she was the Vice President Overseas Operations for the Australian Adoptive Families Association and had every intention of 'escorting 12 proposed adoptees to Australia as soon as possible'. She threatened to create 'unfavourable press' unless her demands were met. Other individuals,

---

100 Barclay is quoted in Marie Toshack, 'Death Faces Vietnam Waifs'. *Sydney Morning Herald,* 13 June 1972: 12.

101 Rosemary Calder, 'Inter-country Adoption from the Point of View of Adoptive Parents'. In *Shaping the Future for our Children,* papers presented at the ICSW Asia and Western Pacific Regional Conference, Melbourne, August 1979: 22.

acting alone or as part of a growing number of activist parent groups, began clamouring to adopt Vietnamese babies. By December 1973 Australian authorities in Saigon reported back to Canberra that certain individuals were stirring up trouble and 'threatening adverse publicity' due to a hold up in processing the cases.[102]

State and Federal parliamentarians tried to satisfy the demands of their constituents who were pressuring for speedy processing of overseas adoptions. In his 1973 address to parliament Tony Staley, the member for Chisholm, proposed a processing centre be established in Saigon to facilitate and expedite adoptions.

> What I am looking for is something like an Australian halfway house in Saigon where someone could be responsible for undertaking all the organisational details, for finding suitable babies for interested Australian couples and, in particular, for cutting through all the incredible red tape that is inevitably bound up in these procedures.[103]

In Saigon tensions emerged between the Australian authorities, intent on caution and due process, and those seeking to fast-track adoptions. In August 1974 the Australian authorities in Saigon complained in a memorandum to Canberra:

> Problems have increased with the arrival in RVN of individual Australian citizens or residents, either attempting to adopt children themselves or acting on behalf of individuals or associations… who are sometimes inclined to adopt 'standover tactics' towards Vietnamese officials to obtain the necessary clearances—even to the extent of smuggling children out of Vietnam… It has also been difficult for us to maintain a calm, reasonable relationship with these Australians who tend to become highly emotional when the Embassy declines to assist them in circumventing authorised procedures.[104]

---

102 The National Archives of Australia holds these records. See cables from the Australian Embassy in Saigon, 24 October 1973 and 14 December 1973. NAA A1838, 3014/10/15/6 PART I, 96 and 41.

103 Tony Staley, Speech to the House of Representatives Grievance debate, 25 October 1973. Commonwealth of Australia: Parliamentary Debates: Official *Hansard*, 2679.

104 Rosemary Calder reported the tensions in 'The Role of the Consumer and Citizen Groups'. In Picton (ed), *Proceedings of the First Australian Conference on Adoption*, 152. The Australian Consul in Saigon made the complaint in a Memorandum on Consular Workload Statistics, 24 August 1974. NAA A1838, 1490/5/74 PART 3, 261–262.

By the beginning of 1975 the political tide was turning, and the Whitlam government was in decline. The fall of Saigon was imminent. The momentum was building for a mass evacuation of personnel and with it came a cry to rescue the 'orphans' of the war. Activists like Mrs Norman Davidson, President of the Australian Adoptive Families Association in New South Wales, pushed the panic button. 'We are grabbing the children while we can get them... Vietnam will fall in three weeks and adoptions will be finished. The Viet Cong will never let orphans leave the country... Vietnam will be closed, just as has happened in Cambodia'. In April 1975 the Australian government reacted decisively. Canberra cabled Saigon: 'The adoption of Vietnamese orphans is a long-standing private expression of Australian concern at the suffering caused by war and the government, with the full support of all segments of the Australian people, is accelerating the movement of orphans'.[105]

Political opportunism underscored by genuine humanitarian concerns saw what became known as Operation Babylift, the evacuation and subsequent adoption of some 280 infants and children from Saigon to Australia in two dramatic airlifts in April 1975. The press had a field day. 'Australia ready for waifs' rang out the *Canberra Times*, 'It was the saddest trip of all', headlined the *Sunday Telegraph*, and the *Sun Herald* recorded that 'Tears greet waifs'. There were critics of the Babylift who saw the removal of children as immoral, claiming that many were not bona fide orphans and that they should be assisted to stay in their country of birth. Speaking through its emissaries in Peking [Beijing], the Provisional Revolutionary Government of South Vietnam accused the Australian government of complicity with the USA in using the pretext of humanitarian aid to kidnap Vietnamese children. But many Australians greeted the mission as a heroic end to a disastrous conflict, a way of redeeming our involvement in a bloody, messy, and illegal war. In this the government and the people were united. When the *Daily Telegraph* announced on 7 April 1975 'Mums Rush Waifs—more on the way', it signalled that the public was primed to secure babies from overseas sources, by whatever means necessary. While Federal and State governments still needed to sort out the legal and political ramifications of bringing in children for the purposes of adoption, the public verdict was in. The effects of the Babylift on intercountry adoption in Australia—and indeed in the First World—would be felt for years to come. Intercountry

---

105   Mrs Davidson is quoted in Janet Hawley, '... Cutting Red Tape for New Citizens'. *The Australian*, 3 April 1975. Outgoing Cablegram, Department of Foreign Affairs to Australian Embassy, Saigon, 4 April 1975. NAA A1209, 1975/546, 119.

adoption could now be seen as a legitimate means of meeting a growing market for babies no longer being sourced by local suppliers.[106]

CONTROLLING THE INTERNATIONAL TRADE IN CHILDREN

'I understood how they felt—I was disappointed, frustrated that I couldn't help them and I was certainly disappointed if they couldn't see that... the system had limitations: "why can't I have a baby tomorrow?"' Peter Fopp was in charge of adoption services in the South Australian Department for Community Welfare between 1974 and 1981. He remembers the atmosphere of chaos and confusion that surrounded the 1975 Saigon Babylift and the impatience of prospective parents as they waited for the babies to be screened, sorted and allocated.

When the new communist government in Vietnam put an end to inter-country adoption, adoption agencies and pro-adoption parent organisations had to look elsewhere for a supply of adoptable babies: 'What are we going to do? Where are we going to go?' Fopp was deeply concerned. His department had worked harmoniously with those parent activists who shared his disquiet over the activities of the adoption entrepreneurs like Rena Briand. Now there were reports of prospective parents turning their attention to South America where, rumour had it, some lawyers were buying and selling babies—including, so it was said, children of 'the disappeared', political victims of repressive regimes. As the decade progressed Fopp and others were disturbed by reports of parents shopping for babies in countries like Sri Lanka, Bangladesh and Taiwan, where natural disasters, political instability or population pressures opened up a ready market. 'Children in Taiwan', Fopp wrote to a colleague there in 1979, 'are being adopted by Australians who contact orphanages, go to your country for a short holiday, and return to Australia with their adopted children'.[107]

---

106 For the arrival of the babies, see *Canberra* Times, 5 April 1975; *Sunday Telegraph* and *Sun Herald*, both 6 April 1975. NAA A1838, 3014/10/15/6 PART 2, 118, 94 and 101. Claude Forell voiced some of the criticisms in his opinion piece 'Baby Airlift Adds Folly to Vietnam's Tragedy'. *The Age*, 17 April, 1975: 8. Allegations of kidnapping were reported by Margaret Jones, 'Australia Kidnapping Waifs—PRG'. *Sydney Morning Herald*, 14 April 1975. NAA A1838, 3014/10/15/6 PART 4, 182.

107 Peter Fopp told his stories to Joshua Forkert in an interview on 15 July 2009; Fopp's letter to Ms Tao Shu-Cheng, 4 October 1972, is in the Fopp Archive, Monash University. Reports of South American malpractice were aired by Sheryle Bagwell, 'When Adoption Can Go Terribly Wrong'. *The Australian*, 11 February 1986, 5.

Fopp strongly disagreed with what he called 'the salvation complex of some people [who] believed that it was their job to rescue orphans from overseas and because they could provide a comfortable healthy life that had to be good for the child'. His primary concern was to stop any international trafficking in children. He was not the only one to press for a more cautious approach to adoption within the whole package of overseas welfare options. Rosemary Calder was a consistent advocate for legislative and administrative reform 'to prevent self-interested parties from taking advantage of loopholes and anomalies in adoption procedures'. As early as September 1973, renowned Australian freelance journalist and cameraman Neil Davis alleged, in an interview on ABC radio, that there were 'buyers of children who travel around the countryside [in Vietnam and Cambodia] paying anything from $10 to $50 for children—just buying them from the mothers in villages'. He later denied that these 'traffickers' were Australian, but claimed that some of the children brought to Australia for adoption had certainly been purchased in this way. Briand, for her part, claimed to have seen no evidence of child trafficking, but countered that although 'the idea of "buying" a child is frowned upon... in Vietnam, what could one do? Let them starve to death?' The contest at this stage was not so much about whether intercountry adoption was a good idea or not, but how adoptions should be arranged and processed and by whom.[108]

Motivated by his personal respect for human life, his sense of social justice, his Christian values and his professional ethic, Fopp dedicated himself to promoting reform of the practice of intercountry adoption in the interests of the adopted children. With the support of the Director-General of his department he worked to resolve differences in practice between the States, to rationalise the responsibilities of States and Commonwealth, and to cut out the entrepreneurs by setting up working relationships with governments in south and south east Asia to implement these adoptions. Fopp believed that a child should be given every opportunity in his/her own country and that intercountry adoption should only take place when responsible authorities were satisfied that adoption overseas was better than all the available internal solutions. In this he continued to have the support of the Council of Social Welfare Ministers and the more responsible parent's

---

108 Cliff Picton and Rosemary Calder, 'Inter-country Adoption Policy in Australia: The Abnegation of Responsibility?' *Australian Child and Family Welfare*, 7(2) (1982): 101. A transcript of the ABC Radio interview with Neil Davis, 29 September 1973, may be found at NAA: A446, 1973/76252. Rena Briand, *The Waifs*. Melbourne: Phuong-Hoang Press, 1973, 56.

groups like the recently formed Australian Society for Intercountry Aid (Children) (ASIAC), but other parent groups chose to work with American agencies whose practices were less ethical.

Slow moving bureaucratic reforms of the kind attempted by Commonwealth and State and Territory governments through the late 1970s and 1980s do not have the excitement and appeal to raw emotion of the media-fired confrontations engineered by individuals such as Moir or Briand, nor the drama of the Babylift. Fopp and others like him worked tirelessly to achieve what they called an 'integrated approach to intercountry adoption' and 'uniform adoption legislation' both across Australia and between Australia and other countries. Working through the intercountry adoption subcommittee of the Victorian Adoption Conference, Graeme Gregory (supported by ASIAC and his Child Care Service) unsuccessfully proposed a national agency to coordinate policy on intercountry adoption.[109] Uniform adoption legislation did exist across Australian States and Territories, but this legislation covered local adoptions only, and efforts to include provisions for intercountry adoption had the effect of introducing inconsistencies. Fopp himself chaired a Commonwealth Inter-departmental Committee on Intercountry Adoption (set up in 1975) and organised workshops dedicated to intercountry adoption at annual conferences of the International Council on Social Welfare. In 1978 and 1979, the Council of Social Welfare Ministers sent bilateral delegations of State and Federal representatives to the eight Asian countries that were then allowing their children to be adopted by Australians. While the delegation did not immediately succeed in achieving formal written agreements with all the countries visited, it found value in the airing of common concerns and approaches.

Diplomacy and reasoned discussion rather than public confrontation were the basis of these efforts to achieve an informed resolution of many legitimate, different approaches and different needs. Ideally Fopp hoped to achieve an international network for intercountry adoption that could be affiliated to the International Council of Social Welfare and eventually, through that organisation, accredited by the United Nations. This did not happen. He did establish and coordinate an International Adoption Network but in the end did not have the resources to keep it going after he left the department. Although some headway was made throughout the latter part of the 1970s,

---

109   Graeme Gregory, Simone Kyatt and Katharine Lancaset, 'Intercountry Adoption—
      Report to the Australian Government Social Welfare Commission on the progress,
      achievements and future of the Intercountry Adoption Sub-Committee of the
      Victorian Adoption Conference', June 1975.

5.1 Elaine Moir was not the first to 'smuggle' babies into Australia. This image shows Henri H. Tovel being loaded into a sack to be smuggled to England and Australia, March 1919. The orphan boy had become the mascot of the No 4 Squadron, Australian Flying Corps, and all agreed to assist in an attempt to smuggle him home to Australia, where he was adopted by a member of the Corps.

Australian War Memorial: A03056, with permission Australian War Memorial.

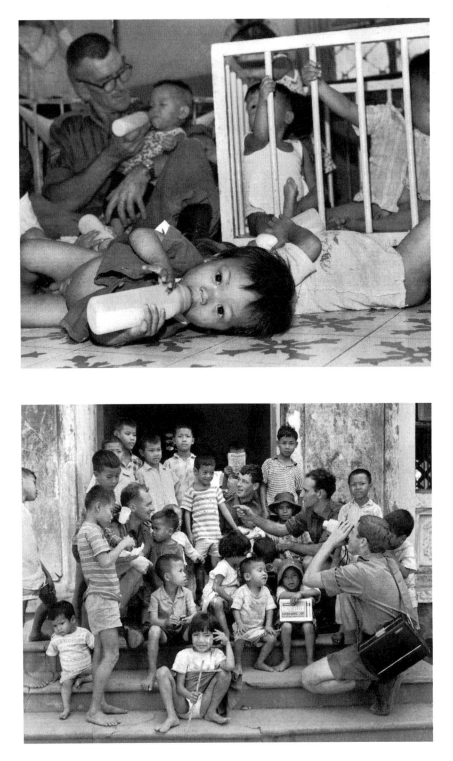

5.2 (left top)   Corporal James Giles, 110th Signal Squadron, spent time with the orphaned children at Don Chua Orphanage. Gia Dinh Province, Saigon, September 1967. Photograph by Michael Coleridge.

Australian War Memorial: COL/67/0752/VN, with permission Australian War Memorial.

5.3 (left bottom)   Soldiers turned film makers are hoping to improve the lives of children at An Phong Orphanage. They are shooting a film in their spare time to draw attention in Australia to the plight of the orphans. Vung Tau, South Vietnam. April 1970. Photograph by John Geoffrey Fairley.

Australian War Memorial: FAI/70/0205/VN, with permission Australian War Memorial.

5.4 (above)   Cao Thi Phuong was one of the first two South Vietnamese orphans to come to Australia, in January 1968, and her story made front-page headlines around the country. Her adoptive father explained that the family viewed their adoption of three-year-old Phuong as "lending a hand" to Australia's war effort in Vietnam. State Library of Victoria Image no hp001397.

Reproduced with permission Newspix (for Herald & Weekly Times Limited).

5.5 (above)   A case of 'all hands to the
bottles' during the second RAAF airlift
of Vietnamese orphans to Australia. Seen
here feeding babies at Tan Son Nhut airfield
were three crew members from 37 Squadron
Saigon, Vietnam, 17 April 1975.
Australian War Memorial: P01973.002, with
permission Australian War Memorial.

5.6–5.8 (right)   The arrival at Mascot,
Sydney, of Vietnamese orphans in
'Operation Babylift'. Government
Printing Office 3–25621, 3–25666, and
3–25640.
Mitchell Library, State Library of New
South Wales, with permission.

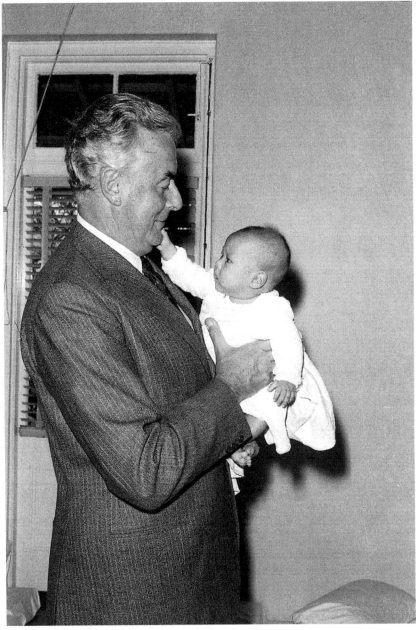

5.9 (above) Australian Labor Prime Minister Gough Whitlam nurses 7-month old Don Hy Vong, at Sydney's North Head quarantine station on 6 April 1975. Whitlam and his wife went to greet some of the 212 Vietnamese waifs flown in on a chartered jumbo jet. *The Age*, 7 April 1975, p. 1. Photograph by K. Berry.

With permission, Fairfax Syndication.

5.10 Bringing adoption out of the closet: A war orphan from Vietnam starts school in Australia, 1970.

National Archives of Australia: A1501, A11167. With permission National Archives of Australia.

5.11 Indigo Williams Willing and Jen Fitzpatrick, 14 August 2005. Indigo Thuy Willing (Huynh Thi Diep Thuy) was adopted by an Australian family in 1972 as part of the adoption of over a hundred Vietnamese war orphans. Jen arrived in Australia from Saigon (now Ho Chi Minh City) on the first Operation Babylift flight on 7 April 1975. Both women are members of Adopted Vietnamese International (AVI) and have done much to assist adult adoptees to reclaim their own stories. Photograph by Reina Irmer.

State Library of Queensland Image number: 6317-0001-0264, with permission.

uniform legislation remained a sticking point as did negotiations between 'sending' and 'receiving' nations.

Writing in 1982 after he had left his position in the South Australian government, Fopp had to admit that, despite these efforts, 'the first thing to be said about Australia's position in intercountry adoption is that there is not one [single position]... '[110] Debate circled around whether responsibility for controlling the 'international trade in children' should rest with the sending or receiving country. A steady stream of media reports alleged rackets in baby stealing and selling overseas. Couples who attempted to bypass the system and 'purchase' a baby in countries like Mexico, Chile and Taiwan were still liable to find that the government would refuse the child an entry visa for Australia. At the same time, the welfare and progress of those children who found themselves at the forefront of Asian migration to Australia in the early 1970s could begin to be measured and the appropriateness of intercountry adoption evaluated. More than that, transracial adult adoptees began to speak in their own voices, reclaiming their history and creating new narratives of their experiences.

PARENTS AND BUREAUCRATS: FROM CONFLICT TO COOPERATION

Deborra-Lee Furness is only the most recent in a long line of adopting parents to condemn what they see as an anti-adoption culture in Australia. Media reports have consistently supported the parents' claim that policy-makers and social welfare practitioners are hostile towards adoption—and especially intercountry adoption. And it is certainly true that in the early decades, some state agencies were more sympathetic than others towards parents wishing to adopt a child from another country. At a national level state and Commonwealth authorities agreed on an aim of eliminating private adoptions and stopping individuals from jumping the queue. But it would be a mistake to view the issue as one involving a simple opposition of parents and parent groups to officialdom.

Intercountry adoption as a global child welfare intervention was born out of disaster; its early history is mostly associated with moments of crisis in sending countries. It was in such situations that the tension between prospective parents with their differing motivations and Australian government agencies became most intense. Government authorities had to address

---

110   Peter Fopp, 'Inter-country Adoption: Australia's Position'. *Australian Journal of Social Issues* 17(1) (1982): 50.

different sets of needs: firstly, the best interests of the child in accordance with international conventions on human rights; secondly, the place of intercountry adoption as part of Australia's total overseas aid program and humanitarian immigration policy; and only finally the needs of infertile couples wishing to establish a family. The reaction of parent advocates could be naively simplistic. John Osborne, president of the group 'Rights for Adoptive Families', wrote of the crisis in Kampuchea in the late 1970s, 'We have then children in desperate need, and couples ready to meet that need. Holding these two areas of love apart is the twentieth century monster—bureaucracy... To the practising Christians of Australia I suggest that shame make your legs falter when next you climb the church's steps unless you act now'.[111]

In the early 1980s intercountry adoption into Australia was driven and largely controlled by the activities of groups of adopting parents. Formed originally for mutual support and to pressure governments and bureaucrats, these groups established direct relationships with orphanages and institutions overseas and developed an expertise in dealing with these organisations that gave them significant influence. This influence was to diminish as Australian Commonwealth, state and territory governments began to develop nationally agreed procedures for intercountry adoption programs.

Tensions arose within and between the advocate groups as they jostled for their share of the market. The earliest group, the Adoptive Families Association, began in 1973 with active branches in South Australia, Victoria and New South Wales, but in 1974 a split in South Australia created an opening for a group originally based in Victoria, the Australian Society for Intercountry Aid (Children). In South Australia, ASIAC became the only accredited adoption agency, developing sponsorship aid programs, assisting prospective parents and contributing to the development of policy within Australia both through discussion and formal submissions to government reviews. As late as 1989 in Victoria, ASIAC was *de facto* managing the Indian overseas adoption program for the State. Fearing diminished influence, several of the parent groups came together to form AICAN (Australian Intercountry Adoption Network), which operates as an umbrella organisation offering support and advice to parents involved in intercountry

---

111 Reprint of a Speech made by John Osborne of Victorian Society for Aiding Refugee Children to a press conference in November 1979 calling for action for Kampuchean children, as included in the March 1980 newsletter of the Rights for Adoptive Families Newsletter, 4.

adoption. In 1990, the year of its foundation, AICAN could claim to represent twenty-one non-accredited parent organisations.[112]

The power of these parents' groups was gradually diminished by changes in the global culture of intercountry adoption and by corresponding developments in Australia's national policy. In 1986 the federal Council of Social Welfare Ministers' national guidelines put two principles concerning adoption in place: that the interests of the child should come first; and that before overseas adoption was considered, suitable forms of care must first be sought in the country of origin. These reflected a draft UN declaration which declared that 'The first priority for a child is to be cared for by his or her own parents'. In 1991, the states, territories and Commonwealth agreed on procedures for the negotiation and approval of new programs, requiring the states and territories to assume responsibility for initiating programs with overseas countries. Policy firmed around the doctrine of finding families for children, not children for families.[113]

There is no question that the transfer of children from one country to another, usually from the developing to the developed world, opens up the possibility of exploitation and fraud, especially when money enters the transaction. Australia has not been immune from recurring allegations of complicity in the illegal trade in children. Aside from the straightforward criminality of child trafficking, a cluster of ambiguities attach themselves to money in relation to intercountry adoption. Within Australia, intercountry adoption is an expensive program to run, involving as it does various diplomatic activities between this country and a number of sending countries. Who should carry the costs? Investigating the provision of services in Victoria after a scandalous mishandling of an Indian adoption in 1989, Justice Fogarty noted that while fees for services were necessary to help cover administrative costs, they created uncertainty around the question of who is the client. Fogarty wrote, 'As the parents are paying out and they are in Victoria and the children are not, it gives rise to a view that the service is for them. It is not'. Then there is the problem of a lack of transparency around donations to foreign organisations that might also offer children for adoption. ASIAC, for example, has from its beginning run aid and sponsorship programs alongside its activities in facilitating adoptions

---

112 For the role and influence of ASIAC, see *Overseas Adoption in Australia*, 94, par 5.24; and Mr Justice J. F. Fogarty, K. Sanders and M. Webster, *A Review of the Intercountry Adoption Service in Victoria.* [Melbourne]: Family and Children's Services Council, October 1989, 85.

113 *Overseas Adoption in Australia*, 39, par 2.69.

through direct contact with orphanages and child care institutions overseas. The Hague Convention on the Protection of Children and Co-operation in Respect of Intercountry Adoption (1993) attempted to deal with this by demanding a separation between the accredited adoption agencies that handled adoption and those administering aid. ASIAC and similar parent groups were therefore by definition excluded from accreditation under the Hague Convention.[114]

Finally, the Hague Convention made it clear that states of origin were to have overarching powers in relation to intercountry adoption. Receiving states which ratify Hague have no role in 'finding' children for intercountry placement, nor in pressuring sending agencies to provide children. Their role is limited to approving suitable families, agreeing to placements and carrying out related professional casework. Since Australia ratified Hague in 1998, the whole process of intercountry adoption has been increasingly structured by legislation. At the time of the Commonwealth parliamentary inquiry into intercountry adoption in 2005, programs were managed by state and territory governments, with each state having 'lead status' for a program with a particular country. This function has now been centralised in the Commonwealth Attorney-General's Department, which also ensures compliance with international protocols. State and territory Central Authorities process individual adoption applications and supervise placements. Committed parents groups still have a valued role to play, but this is confined to consultation, pre-adoption education and post-adoption support.[115]

Advocates for adopting parents continue to insist that intercountry adoption is a positive way of forming families, preferable to institutional life in the child's country of birth. But since the early 1990s their advice to intending parents also acknowledges some of the difficulties of intercountry adoption. Parents are urged to give something back to the country of origin—to support an orphanage there, or a program to help children to stay with their birth families. AICAN's formal endorsement of international conventions such as the UN Convention on the Rights of the Child (1989) and the Hague Convention on... Intercountry Adoption (1993) is a measure

---

114 Justice Fogarty's views on fees for services may be found in his report *A Review of the Intercountry Adoption Service in Victoria*, 41, par. 2.

115 The role of the receiving states under Hague are explained by Helen Bayes, 'Let's Consider the Issues': Intercountry Adoption in Tasmania 1993, A discussion paper, 12-15, par. 7 (citing Fogarty). The 'lead State' concept is described and illustrated in *Overseas Adoption in Australia*, 42, pars 2.72 to 2.75 and table 2.2.

of the journey taken, at least nominally, by intercountry adoption advocates. The personal interests of adopting parents are counterbalanced by official insistence that intercountry adoption has to be controlled in order to protect vulnerable birth families in times of disaster, and to prevent the abduction, exploitation, sale and trafficking of children.

BECOMING A TRANSNATIONAL ADOPTIVE PARENT

Intercountry adoption has always taken place in the shadow of the colonial past and of present inequalities of wealth and power.[116] Why do parents choose to adopt a child from another country, another culture, another race? How do they address the challenges of raising such a child and deal with issues of identity that cross national boundaries? Three stories from the History of Adoption website highlight some of these issues.

When Emma Anderson, already the mother of two sons, embarked upon the notion of adopting a child from Ethiopia as a means of extending her family, she was driven by humanitarian concern and a strong Christian faith. When Emma was finally able to adopt a young daughter from Ethiopia, she named her Grace, and refers to her as a 'gift' and a 'miracle' from God.

Liz Peter's search for a baby overseas was the direct result of her inability to conceive a child of her own. Attempts at IVF failed, and the queue for local babies was impossibly long. The process of adopting a child from overseas was also long and difficult, and Liz is scathing in her criticism of the bureaucrats involved. Eventually Liz was able to adopt a five-year old boy from Thailand, whom she renamed Samuel.

'The process is the issue I'd like to talk about', says Marian Jacobs, mother of two children adopted from the Philippines. Marian points her finger at the government authorities whom she sees as being deliberately obstructionist and unhelpful. 'We received no help from the department. Not during and not after the process'. Marian acknowledges the cultural problems of intercountry adoption, but brushes them aside. Clearly she accepts that all the children put up for adoption are unwanted and abandoned.

> I believe ultimately it would be the best for the children if they could have stayed with their birth parents in their home country. But we all

---

116 The shadow of the colonial past idea is introduced in Submission No 183, from the Department of Community Development, Government of Western Australia to the HRSCHFS *Inquiry into Adoption of Children from Overseas*, 24 May 2005, 10.

know that the reality of poverty, relinquishment and abandonment create a situation where it is best for the child to be raised by a loving family.

Humanitarianism is often cited as the main factor moving parents to adopt from overseas. Certainly this motive justified the practice in its early days. Parents still cite a hope to 'make a difference' as a reason for adopting from overseas, especially when they already have children of their own. Michael and Danielle Potter explained to a government inquiry that

> We were told that we were wasting our time adopting African children. The problem was too big. We agree that we can't solve the whole problem. However, we have made a difference for two children and that's worth everything.

But while parents link adoption to a concern for the wellbeing of children the world over, it is always coupled with a desire to create or complete a family of one's own. 'Overseas adoption gives a couple the opportunity to become a family and gives the adoptive child the opportunity to live a happy life and a future they would never have the opportunity to receive'.[117]

At the same time parents have come to understand something of the cultural implications of overseas adoption. 'You don't just take on another child, but take on a child of other people, another country'. Most make some attempt to keep their children 'in touch' with the culture of their birth, but few have a deep understanding of that culture. A recent study of thirty five adopting parents in Queensland found that all 'attempted to acknowledge and incorporate various aspects of the birth heritage of adoptees into their lives'. Activities ranged from dress-up parties to regular trips back to the child's country of birth. The study found that while these activities changed the lives of the adopting families in many positive ways, 'issues of race and power' limited the possibility of real transformation. Being a transnational adopting parent is a transformational act, but more for the parent than for the child being adopted. These parents feel they are becoming 'citizens of the world'. In the words of one participant, 'we're the lucky ones'.

> I mean what's lucky about coming into the world and being taken away from your birth mother and then having to move to another

---

117 Submission no. 27 from Michael and Danielle Potter, to the HRSCHFS *Inquiry into Adoption of Children from Overseas*, 19 April 2005; Submission no. 15 from Carolyn Bird, to the HRSCHFS *Inquiry into Adoption of Children from Overseas*, 19 April 2005.

country? To me I can't see that he's lucky. I think we're lucky because he's our child and we can give him a wonderful life and whatever.

These parents also have an honest appreciation of the limits of their generosity. One noted that given 'the cost of adopting a child, and raising a child in Australia… you could help around sixty children in Ethiopia for ten years or so, through World Vision… If you really want to rescue children, adoption really isn't the most effective way'.[118]

THE DECLINE OF INTERCOUNTRY ADOPTION

Since the 1970s, children have been adopted to Australia from seventy countries, 80 per cent of them in Asia, and 86 per cent of them from ten principal sending countries: Korea, Sri Lanka, India, the Philippines, China, Thailand, Vietnam, Ethiopia, Columbia and Chile. Transnational adoptions have outnumbered domestic adoptions since 1999. Between 1970 and 2008, 10,221 children arrived in Australia as intercountry adoptees.

An analysis of annual government statistics on adoption shows that intercountry adoption to Australia occurred in three main waves, determined by push and pull factors inside and outside the country. The first wave was triggered by concerns for child orphans during the Vietnam War in the early 1970s. These children found themselves at the spearhead of Asian migration to Australia as the so-called White Australia Policy was dismantled. The abandonment of restrictive immigration by the end of the 1970s allowed the establishment of formal ICA programs with a range of Asian countries, as well as countries in South America, Africa and Eastern Europe. Korea was the largest program of the second wave. It was anticipated that Australia's 1998 ratification of the Hague Convention on… Intercountry Adoption would lead to a rapid expansion of programs and increase ICA arrivals. This increase did not eventuate as imagined. Instead, paradoxically, the third wave of arrivals resulted from the opening in 1999 of a bilateral program with China, at that stage a non-Hague Convention country.

After peaking in 2004–2005, the number of intercountry adoptions has steadily declined in Australia as in the world generally. Globally,

---

118 The child of another country caution comes from *Overseas Connections News*, Newsletter of Community Services Victoria Vol. 1 (Spring 1991). Indigo Anne Williams Willing, who was herself adopted as a child from Vietnam, has studied transracial adoptions extensively. The quotations included here are from her thesis, *Transnational Adoption and Constructions of Identity and Belonging: A Qualitative Study of Australian Parents of Children Adopted from Overseas*. PhD thesis, School of Social Science, University of Queensland, 2010, 204, 159 and 158.

intercountry adoptions have fallen from more than 45,000 in 2004 to 29,000 in 2010. In the decade from 2001 to 2011 most Australian intercountry adoptions were sourced from China (787 children) and South Korea (712 children), but numbers have dropped away from both countries: China sent 125 children to Australia in 2006–2007, but only 51 in 2010; Korea sent 103 in 2005–2006 but only 19 in 2010–2011. These declining numbers are mirrored by a fall in the number of children available from Australia's other regular suppliers. Intercountry adoption continues to represent the dominant category of adoptions in the first decade of the twenty-first century. But that same decade has seen the lowest total number of adoptions since national data have been collected.[119]

The falling numbers of intercountry adoptions is no indication of any lack of demand for adoptable children within the Australian population; it indicates lack of supply. And just as the failure of supply on the domestic market in the 1970s moved would-be parents to explore the adoption market overseas, so this current 'crisis' in supply has generated a new source of supply—the surrogacy market.

---

119 Information on the numbers of intercountry and local adoptions has been gathered from three sources: Trudy Rosenwald, 'Ten Thousand Journeys: A Brief Demographic Survey of Intercountry Adoption in Australia'. In Spark and Cuthbert (eds.), *Other People's Children*, 197–206; Peter Selman, 'The Global Decline of Intercountry Adoption: What Lies Ahead?' *Social Policy and Society* 11(3), (2012): 381–397; Australian Institute of Health and Welfare (AIHW), annual report *Adoptions Australia 2010–2011*, 52, Table A10: Intercountry adoptions by country of origin, 2001–2002 to 2010–2011.

CHAPTER 6

NEW FRONTIERS

In March 2009 the *Age* newspaper in Melbourne carried an article by Sharon Grey with the headline 'Does it matter where babies come from?' It tells the story of the birth of Matthew and Rachel's child, by international surrogacy.

> Matthew and Rachel longed for a child, but after five years of IVF treatments, as well as hypnotherapy, psychotherapy, counselling, Chinese medicine, exploratory laparoscopy, hysteroscopy and other procedures, they finally accepted that conception was not going to happen.

The couple turned to intercountry adoption. 'They completed the required education, passed intensive scrutiny by a social worker and received approval 18 months later, only to be told that they may need to wait up to five years'. Grey quotes Matthew: 'It's a failed system'.

The next option was surrogacy. Matthew and Rachel found a clinic in Mumbai 'and suddenly felt very comfortable'. The clinic provided IVF and surrogacy services, mostly to Indian customers. While controversy surrounds offshore surrogacy and its exploitation of poor women, Grey puts another view: surrogate mothers are well treated and anonymous.

> Surrogates are not poverty-stricken village women. They come from the lower-middle classes, are married with children and remain virtually anonymous to the parents... For her service the woman [who carried Matthew and Rachel's child] received around $10,000, the equivalent of five years' wages—enough to change her family's life and educate her children. She does not nurse the infant.

Rachel told Grey; 'I was in Aldi buying nappies when I got the call telling me our baby had arrived three weeks early... We left for India five days later'. Completing the paperwork was much more difficult than taking possession of their child.

'DNA testing had to be done in Australia and the bureaucracy was just incredible. Australia does not make this easy', says Rachel, as she cradles her sweet, sleeping son.

Matthew and Rachel were the first Australians to achieve parenthood via an Indian surrogate mother. Since 2009 many infertile couples have followed their path from IVF to intercountry adoption and on to surrogacy. Sharon Grey's opinion piece contrasts the sweet, sleeping baby in Rachel's arms against what are described as systemic failures in the intercountry adoption process, and the 'incredible' bureaucratic obstacles put in the paths of parents of children born overseas to surrogate mothers.

What could be more simple or wonderful, Grey seems to be asking, than this scene of familial bliss with the loving parents and Luke, their sweet baby son? Why should the Australian government and bureaucracy make it so hard for people who long for children to have a baby of their own? This juxtaposition of heartless bureaucracy and the natural desire of couples to have a baby of their very own to love and nurture has long been a feature of debates on adoption—as we saw in Chapter 5, it has characterised public debate on intercountry adoption in Australia since the time of the baby lift of supposed orphans from Saigon in 1975. Grey is impatient with bureaucracy: her article challenges the seemingly senseless delays and obstacles placed in the paths of parents such as Matthew and Rachel. Thus, she asks, when we see this happy family scene, does it really matter where the baby comes from?[120]

How we respond to this last question depends on whose viewpoint we take. For the parents who long for a child of their own, the question of where the baby comes from may come to matter when the baby grows to maturity and seeks information about the mother who gave birth to him. Equally, as we have learned from the history of adoption, for parents the question of the origins of their child—much wanted as an infant—may emerge as a pressing issue as the child matures and the conflicts of adolescence set in. Beyond individual viewpoints, there are larger ethical and social issues which we as a community need to address. Do we really believe that the provision of children to prospective loving parents is such a self-evident and overwhelming good that it doesn't matter where the babies come from? Versions of this question have driven moral, ethical and political debates about adoption for all of its history and now in the first decade of this century

---

120 Matthew and Rachel's story is retold by Sharon Grey, 'Does It Matter Where Babies Come From?' *The Age*, 11 March 2009. http://www.theage.com.au/opinion/does-it-matter-where-babies-come-from-20090310-8u80.html

the same question arises with respect to surrogate births. Surrogacy in both altruistic and, particularly, commercial forms appears to be taking the place of adoption as a way of making families. We return to this issue here as we explore the emergence of surrogacy.

INTERCOUNTY ADOPTION: A FAILED SYSTEM?

As yet, we have little firm data on the numbers of children being commissioned by Australian parents through commercial surrogacy arrangements overseas, in places including India, Thailand and the United States. The data we have indicate that this is a rapidly growing phenomenon, already outstripping intercountry adoption as a way of making families for Australians unable to conceive naturally or through assisted reproductive technologies. *The Age* reported in June 2012 that the numbers of offshore surrogate births to Australian commissioning parents are growing dramatically: from 97 births in 2009 to 269 in 2011. By contrast, Australian Institute of Health and Welfare data on adoptions show a continuing decline in the numbers of intercountry adoptions in Australia, down to 149 in 2012. It seems that intercountry adoption is in decline, in Australia and worldwide.[121]

The drop in adoptions and the emerging evidence of the rise in offshore surrogacy strongly suggests that the market in children has shifted from intercountry adoption with its decreasing numbers of young and healthy infants globally, to a different form of market: an offshore and web-based market in eggs, sperms, and wombs. The new market relies in equal measures on advanced reproductive technologies and old fashioned inequalities in wealth and power. As American adoption historians Diana Marre and Laura Briggs write compellingly, examining the flows in the trade in babies or in the case of surrogacy, the trade in eggs, sperm and wombs tells us a lot about power and influence, and about poverty and marginalisation.[122] Overwhelmingly the flow in babies has been from the poor to the affluent.

---

121 Anna Whitelaw, 'Hundreds Pay for Overseas Surrogacy'. *The* Age, 3 June 2012. http://www.theage.com.au/opinion/political-news/hundreds-pay-for-overseas-surrogacy-20120602-1zp1u.html *Lateline*, 5 March 2013, claimed almost 400 babies were born to Australians using Indian surrogates in 2011. For Australian Institute of Health and Welfare data, see *Adoptions Australia 2010–2011* (Canberra: Australian Institute of Health and Welfare, 2011), 14; and *Adoptions Australia 2011–2012*, vi. Peter Selman, 'The Global Decline of Intercountry Adoption: What Lies Ahead?'. *Social Policy and Society* 11(3) (2012): 381–397.

122 Diana Marre and Laura Briggs, *International Adoption: Global Inequalities and the Circulation of Children*. New York: NYU Press, 2009.

Likewise, affluent women in developed countries are not hiring out their wombs for the gestation of other people's children: this labour is concentrated in the poorer parts of the world.

In their quest to have a baby of their own, Matthew and Rachel found intercountry adoption to be a failed system. For couples and individuals desperate to make a family for themselves, intercountry adoption fails to deliver babies or young children within acceptable time frames. Stories posted on government and research websites stress the sheer anguish of waiting. Couples spend years hoping to conceive naturally, years more attempting through IVF, then as long again waiting for approval to adopt and then to receive a child of their own through intercountry adoption, with some so-called paper pregnancies lasting upwards of five years. If intercountry adoption is seen primarily as a service for those seeking children to adopt— and despite the best efforts of state and territory departments to put a different view, this is certainly how it has come to be perceived by many Australians—it is understandable that these delays are seen as intolerable and the mark of a failed system.

If, on the other hand, intercountry adoption is seen primarily as a service to children for whom other more acceptable care options are unavailable or have been exhausted, the delays in accessing adoptable children from overseas may be understood in another light. What looks like intolerable delay and inhumane bureaucracy may look quite different when viewed through the lens of Australia's obligations under the Hague Convention on Protection of Children and Co-operation in Respect of Intercountry Adoption. In addition to ensuring that children for adoption are sourced from approved orphanages in Hague compliant countries, the federal government must be able to certify that the child is genuinely in need of adoption and no other care options are available within the country of origin.

Grey's article cited the exasperation of Matthew, the intending father, at the fact that 'there are about 1000 orphanages in India, but Victoria deals with just five of them'. A view that puts first Australia's obligations under Hague might observe that only a handful of these orphanages satisfy Australian requirements with respect to the origins of the children, their freedom from trafficking, and their legitimate status as adoptable. Recent reports of unwitting Australian complicity in the unlawful adoption of stolen Indian children emphasise the need for caution. As quoted in a 2009 ABC News report, one lawyer claimed that out of the 400 or so Indian children who found new homes in Australia in the past fifteen years, at least 30 were stolen from their birth families. The scandal that broke in 2009 was still festering in 2013, as one of the Indian families demanded the return of their child.[123]

Another source of the increasing queues for intercountry children is that sending countries are putting in place better care and welfare arrangements, meaning that fewer children are finding their way onto the adoption market. Even in countries where there is no strong local culture of adoption and standards of institutional care are seen to be low, governments are moving to restrict the export of children. In December 2012, Russian President Vladimir Putin signed into law a measure that banned the adoption of Russian children by US families as from 1 January 2013. Russian politicians said it was an embarrassment that the country could not care for its own, and supporters of the Bill, politically motivated though it may have been, argued that it would help stimulate reform and domestic adoptions.[124]

In late June 2012, the Commonwealth Attorney-General's Department announced the closure of Australia's intercountry adoption program with Ethiopia. The Ethiopian program has offered hope of a supply of young children for adoption in the face of declining supply from other sending countries such as China and Korea. The terms of the Attorney-General's communique highlight the distance the government sees between the interests of children in Ethiopia and the needs and interests of Australian adoptive parents:

> Ethiopian children in need increasingly have alternative long-term care options made available to them in Ethiopia. The Australian Government supports the Ethiopian Government's efforts to pursue the best interests of their children by facilitating domestic adoptions, long-term foster care arrangements and assisting families in crisis.

The communiqué offers no comfort to Australians on waiting lists for Ethiopian children.

> Unfortunately for prospective adoptive parents outside Ethiopia, this means that it is likely that there will be fewer children referred for intercountry adoption.[125]

---

123 'Australian families caught up in India adoption scandal'. ABC News, 23 February 2009. At http://www.abc.net.au/news/2009-02-22/australian-families-caught-up-in-india-adoption/304668, accessed March 2013. Michael Edwards, 'Indian Family Demands Australian Authorities Return Adopted Girl'. ABC 7.30, 21 February 2013. http://www.abc.net.au/7.30/content/2013/s3695695.htm

124 'Russia's Putin signs anti-US adoption bill'. CNN, 29 December 2012. At http://edition.cnn.com/2012/12/28/world/europe/russia-us-adoptions

125 Attorney-General's website, 30 June 2012.

Thus what looks like a failed system, to Australians seeking children to adopt, might be a system delivering greater benefits to children and families within sending countries, as in the Ethiopian example. These considerations take us back to the question: does it matter where babies come from? Another question may be framed: does the desire to access children to parent, and the ability to provide these children with material benefits not available in their countries of birth, necessarily override the interests of children themselves, their families and communities of origin?

SURROGACY AS A SOLUTION TO THE LATEST 'CRISIS' IN ADOPTION

During the 1970s a decline in the number of adoptable babies available in Australia coincided with the beginnings of large scale intercountry adoption. The decline in the early 2000s in the numbers of babies and very young children available for intercountry adoption has seen a corresponding rise in the pursuit of surrogacy as a way of making families. Co-parenting, where friends co-operate in the conceiving, bearing and rearing of shared children, is probably many times more prevalent than surrogacy, but this raises rather different problems which are not our concern here.[126]

There are notable parallels and contrasts between these two periods of decline in the numbers of children available for adoption. In both cases, decline led to a change in the market; and in both cases, the decreasing numbers of adoptable infants and young children has been described as a crisis. In both cases, the demand for children forged a new market which both reflected and played some part in shifting prevalent views about family. The move to intercountry adoption from the mid-1970s quite dramatically made adoption visible in ways that it previously was not, and challenged mono-cultural views of both family and nation. In the 1960s the success of the adoptive placement was measured in terms of its invisibility: blonde children matched with fair haired parents. This seamless insertion of the adopted child into the adoptive family was upheld by adoption professionals as the pre-condition for successful adoptive families. In stark contrast the intercountry adoptive family visibly declares itself to be a family formed outside biology and across racial and cultural lines. Thus it challenges views about what constitutes an adoptable child, what constitutes a family and what constitutes an Australian citizen, expanding received definitions and assumptions across all of these fronts.

---

126   Information from Rodney Chiang Cruise, by email 13 May 2013.

The growing numbers of off-shore surrogacy arrangements are likewise presenting challenges to received orthodoxies about family. A key market for off-shore surrogacy arrangements is gay male couples, a category express-ly excluded from adoption in most Australian states and territories. The inclusion of gay and lesbian people, and single people, in the category of par-ent represents a challenge to dominant heterosexual norms and the family as the preserve of this norm. A recent court decision in Western Australia allowed the male partner of the father of surrogate twins to adopt the children as a step-parent. The judge, citing the best interests of the children, granted the petitioner a dispensation from requirements under Western Australian law that cleared the way for him to adopt. Her decision signalled a further step towards an expanded recognition of 'the reality of "family" in present day society'.[127]

A further parallel between the market shifts of the 1970s and the 2010s is that on each occasion, the shift was to a model of adoption which provided some advantages to prospective parents over the previous model. The move from local to intercountry adoption from the mid-1970s, while prompted by the downturn in local babies, also allowed Australian adoptive families to escape the impact of adoption reform which re-shaped local adoption over the next two decades. For adoptive parents who felt uncomfortable with the degrees of openness allowed for under the reformed adoption laws, intercountry adoption offered the clean break and exclusive possession of the child that had previously been the norm in the period of secret and sealed adoptions in the years following the Second World War.

Similarly, surrogacy offers something over and above intercountry adopt-ion. The Gay Dads Australia website recommends surrogacy because of 'the difficulties associated with adoption in contemporary society'. For gay men, the advantages of surrogacy over adoption are clear: currently, with the exception of a few Australian states, adoption in not an option for family formation open to homosexual men. In addition, surrogacy allows prospect-ive parents to bypass the difficulties of international adoption and the chall-enge of parenting a child of a different race. Not stated here, but implicit, is the fact that partial or gestational surrogacy—where a woman is implanted with an embryo which contains none of her genetic material—allows for a genetic connection between the child and one or both of the commissioning parents. Surrogacy may proceed with donated sperm and eggs (sourced from

---

127 The judgement was reported by Amanda Banks, 'Gay Man Wins Right to Adopt'. *West Australian*, 25 January 2013. At http://au.news.yahoo.com/thewest/a/-/breaking/15949942/gay-man-wins-right-to-adopt/

an array of internet sites in which details of donors' physical and intellectual characteristics are catalogued for maximum consumer choice); or with the sperm or eggs of both parents; the sperm of one; or the eggs of one. This genetic connection is something that adoption cannot provide, for all of its legal fiction of the child being as if born to the adoptive parents.

The current 'crisis' in adoption seems to have occasioned another change in the market and a new market model for alternative family formation. This crisis terminology begs the question of crisis for whom? That a fall in the numbers of children available for adoption might be framed as a crisis highlights the centring of adoption practices in Australia on the needs of prospective parents in securing access to children for family formation. The shift to surrogacy which is currently taking place in Australia and elsewhere further highlights the parent-centred perspectives at work in many discussions of adoption and family formation. While it is possible in the case of adoption to present arguments about the benefits to the child—which may mask or at least put to the side the interests of the adoptive parents in adoption—no such narratives are available in defence or support of surrogacy. Surrogate birth arrangements do not rescue children from poverty or institutionalisation; the child is commissioned expressly for family formation. Without the surrogacy arrangement, there is no child. Surrogacy is now being spoken of widely as an alternative to the allegedly failed system of adoption, or as adoption perfected, because it delivers something that adoption in most cases fails to deliver. The particular features of surrogacy—as distinct from adoption—offer a clear insight into the operation of this market, untethered from the narratives of child rescue and humanitarianism which have tended to obscure the market elements at work throughout its history. It is to these features which we now turn.

A NEW MARKET IN CHILDREN FOR NEW KINDS OF PARENTS

Australia has laws which prohibit the transaction of commercial surrogate arrangements and allow, under tightly controlled conditions, altruistic (non-commercial) surrogacy. Figures show only 19 children born through altruistic surrogacy arrangements in Australia in 2011. As with the processes of qualifying as an adoptive parent, prospective parents find the processes associated with qualifying for altruistic surrogacy in Australia burdensome and demeaning: 'If they feel like you aren't the right kind of person or if you don't have the right paperwork, you are knocked back. You are treated like a criminal from the start'. An even greater obstacle is finding someone to carry the child for nine months. Commercial surrogacy is legal in the United States and some European countries, but it costs many tens of thousands of dollars to pay surrogates for their time and risk at the rates demanded by an advanced economy. Time, labour and risk are costed at far lower rates in the developing world, so many Australians and other affluent westerners are turning to surrogates in the developing world to bear their children for them.[128]

There are advantages—as described by satisfied consumers—to this new market model. Paying for the services of a surrogate in the developing world provides clarity to the relationship. The purely commercial terms of the transaction help to remove potential emotional complications, as one contributor to a surrogacy blog comments:

> I really believe this is a terrific opportunity for those who are on their last legs trying to have a family. Obviously, this is not for all, and some who are lucky, may find a surrogate within Australia. Speaking with a paediatrician recently, he actually thought offshore commercial surrogacy (Gestational) was probably a better outcome than domestically, for the one reason, being, the Indian child bearer, would be so unlikely wanting to keep the child. The risk in the US and here of course, is the distinct possibility (it happens) that the birth mother suddenly decides she wants to retain the baby and nurture him/her.[129]

The unlikelihood of the Indian surrogate actually wanting to keep the child and burdening herself with one more mouth to feed delivers a better outcome in the view of this consumer and her paediatrician. Stories promoting surrogacy always stress that these women are well paid for their labour—well enough to provide for their own children, who reassuringly remain their focus while they bear children for others.

There are strong indicators that this is a booming market. In late 2011, JOY 94.9 FM, a Melbourne radio station servicing the gay and lesbian community, hosted the 8th Surrogacy for Gay Men Community Forum. Rodney Chiang-Cruise reports on the event:

---

128   Sam Everingham, president of Surrogacy Australia, quoted in Whitelaw, 'Hundreds Pay for Overseas Surrogacy'. The numbers of altruistic surrogate births are also from Whitelaw.

129   Essential Baby website, available at: http://www.essentialbaby.com.au/forums/lofiversion/index.php/t654643.html

Some guys had already started the journey to fatherhood but the majority were just beginning and this forum was their first step along the road to becoming a dad. The forum... has grown from a handful of gay men 8 years ago to a room busting at the seams... As one of the organisers, I was excited and impressed with the number of gay men who are keen to become dads. The word is out to the gay community in Australia. You can be a father, you can pursue that dream of parenthood. Being gay is not a barrier.

Chiang-Cruise believes that the popularity of the forum

comes from the fact that our families are now so visible to the gay and straight community. Our families and our stories are in newspapers, on television, on radio. From the SBS documentary 'Two Men and a Baby' 8 years ago about Tony and Lee, a Melbourne couple who created their family via surrogacy to more recently, Adrian and his partner Ralph who bravely and publicly took the GLBTI community through the pregnancy and birth of their two gorgeous children on the Andy and Adrian breakfast show on JOY 94.9.[130]

To be able to parent their own children, and pursue that dream of parenthood represents a significant and highly symbolic milestone in the quest for equality with the straight community. The real and passionate desire of many gay men to have a family is translated into a platform for political action—the desire for children and family, in the way that heterosexual couples can access them, becomes an issue of equality and rights. This logic underpins the outrage by the gay community in Queensland and elsewhere at the announcement by the Queensland government in June 2012 that it intended to amend legislation in that state to prevent gay men and couples from becoming parents by that route.[131]

The statement by the Queensland government is a piece of predictable homophobia, but we should not allow the issue of gay versus heterosexual rights in debates on surrogacy and adoption (and access to reproductive technologies) to divert attention—as they do—from a more fundamental question of interest, rights and responsibilities. Simply put, no one has a

---

130   Rodney Chiang-Cruise, Co-Moderator, Gay Dads Australia, 'Surrogacy for Gay Men Forum—Report'. http://chiang-cruise.com/?p=779

131   In January 2013, The Queensland government announced its plans to make it illegal for gay couples and single people to use surrogates to have children, a move backed by Christian and conservative groups. http://au.news.yahoo.com/thewest/a/-/national/15777503/gay-surrogacy-ban-breaches-rights/

right to a child. Desire for a child—no matter how powerful, no matter how pervasive—does not and should not be seen to underpin a right to a child. The existence of technologies to enable parenthood, coupled with the persistence of markets in babies, wombs and reproductive labour, do nothing to advance the moral right of any individual to a child. As we move further into this brave new world of commodified children and reproduction, very serious attention needs to be paid to the question posed earlier: does it matter where babies come from?

CONCLUSION

Offshore commercial surrogacy offers, or seemed to offer, a 'terrific opportunity' for those like Matthew and Rachel who are 'on their last legs trying to have a family'. It also offers the only option available for some—gay couples, single men and women, and those too old to qualify as adoptive parents—to form a family. Commercial surrogacy offers clean break adoption, with the commissioning parents and the child under no obligation to have any ongoing contact with the birth mother. Surrogacy also provides potentially more than adoption can give. At best adoption allows the adoptive parent access to other people's children. Surrogacy offers the possibility of a genetic connection to the baby. It remains to be seen, however, how recent changes to India's commercial surrogacy laws, which exclude singles, gay and de facto heterosexual couples from commissioning surrogate babies, will impact on this utopian situation, and whether other countries will follow India's lead into stricter regulation of the surrogacy market.[132]

In the current shift to offshore surrogacy, the needs of commissioning parents are placed clearly front and centre. Surrogacy looks set to take the place of adoption in the early twenty-first century as the newest model in the market for children. The terms of this market actually make clear elements which are obscured in the earlier model of adoption. This market freely declares itself as such, with the commercial elements expunging emotional complications. Birth mothers become gestational carriers who are paid well for their labours.

Further, the move to offshore commercial surrogacy unmasks consumer demand and consumer power and prerogatives. Consumer demand alone drives this market: 'The word is out to the gay community in Australia.

---

132 Kerry Brewster, 'Surrogacy laws may leave Australian babies stateless'. *Lateline*, 5 March 2013. http://www.abc.net.au/news/2013-03-05/surrogacy-laws-could-leave-australian-babies-stateless/4552460

You can be a father, you can pursue that dream of parenthood'. Similarly prospective parent groups which had focused on accessing children through intercountry adoption are now re-orienting their information and support to parenthood via surrogacy.

Prospective parents in the affluent developed worlds have the spending power to shift the focus of the market from adoption to offshore surrogacy; to identify and facilitate new sources of babies for family formation. The earlier market transformation from local to intercountry adoption was accompanied by a shift in what might be considered an adoptable child, with visible difference gaining acceptance. The current transformation of the market—which is a market not in babies, but in wombs and eggs and sperm for the purpose of making babies—is marked by a widening of the types of people who qualify to be classified as parents. But for all these demographic transformations—different types of children, expanded classifications of parents—one thing remains unchanged. Time intensive and risky reproductive labour is still borne by women with far less power than the prospective parents they service. The offshore surrogacy marketplace remains a buyer's market—the prize being the priceless and highly commodified child.

CONCLUSION

This book began with stories from people who experienced adoption in the decades when it was administered as a service to childless couples, and contact between birth families and adoptive families was forbidden. It ends with a story about how a new form of adoption can work today, within an administrative framework that aims to keep birth families together, and promotes openness between birth families and those who have adopted.

Helen (as she chooses to be called) is no ordinary mother. She has birthed and raised four children, fostered about sixteen, and adopted and raised three. But then, the new style of adoption requires qualities of mind, heart and soul that few ordinary mothers possess.

In 1992 Helen and her husband moved into a new home in a small coastal town in Victoria. Five months later her husband died, suddenly and unexpectedly. 'There I was with a house full of new furniture. My children were grown up and living independently. I felt pretty useless'. Then she saw a program on day-time television about foster care, and she thought 'I could do that!' She approached the Department of Human Services, underwent a series of checks and interviews and home visits, and was accepted as an accredited foster parent.

She was first asked to take charge of two young sisters, aged three and four. Helen met with their grandparents, their current foster parents and a social worker, to mutually decide if the placement was suitable. The girls had had nine previous foster homes. Helen listened to the discussion, and heard only negatives about the children. Nobody had a good word for them, and that decided her to take them: 'Every child has something good about them'. At first the girls' behaviour was 'quite poor'. They were not used to stability, 'to having the same bed, the same routine'. And they didn't know what the boundaries were. But they learned quickly, once 'they knew that I loved them'.

Right from the first Helen brought up the girls 'as if they were my own children', though she knew they were not: the fostering arrangement required access visits to their birth parents. These were not successful; the girls did not want to visit, and came home upset and unsettled. After about a year Helen consulted a departmental psychologist, who decided that the visits were 'detrimental to their emotional stability' and had them stopped. Contact continued with the girls' grandparents, with shared Christmas and birthday celebrations.

Victorian law provides for a form of placement known as permanent care. After two years of fostering children, carers can apply to become their legal guardians until they reach the age of eighteen. Orders for permanent care are only made where the birth family is unable to support the child, and ties with the birth family remain open. Permanent care has almost replaced formal adoption in Victoria as a way of placing children who are in need of family and security. Helen applied for a permanent care order as soon as this was possible, and she and the girls celebrated with dinner at McDonalds.

Helen fostered other children during this time, sometimes for weeks, sometimes months. Some were tiny babies, others the same age as her two girls; the family circle expanded easily to take them in; 'we always had plenty of clothes'. Some were particularly needy, and Helen would have liked to keep them. One little girl stayed a year, and then went with her mother to Queensland. Her mother used to ring, and ask Helen to talk to her daughter; the little girl would cry, and ask to come back. Helen went to the department for help; she was told to go home and change her telephone number. So she did— 'but it's not right, it's not natural'.

Three years after she adopted her girls, Helen took in a four-year old boy whose foster parents did not want him. He was a 'bit difficult' at first—at kindergarten he destroyed toys and scared the other children—but within two weeks 'he came good'. Helen treated him—and all the others—like her own child; 'they were not foster children to me, just children'. She wanted them to grow up with no sense that they were different from other children. This wasn't easy; fostering could have 'lots of politics in it'. The four-year old came to her with a mullet hairdo—very long on top—marking him as different to the other kids. Strictly speaking Helen needed his mother's permission to change his haircut, but knowing that she wouldn't get it, she went ahead anyway. The only way she could get him to sit still for the hairdresser was to give him an envelope to put the hair in, so that he could take it to kindergarten to show the teacher. Two years later he too came under her guardianship on a permanent care order.

All three of Helen's charges are grown-up now, and all three are working in good jobs and living in happy relationships. Their paths haven't always been smooth, and Helen is immensely proud of what they have achieved. She is also quietly proud that she 'gave them the start that they needed'. But she insists that 'they were as good for me as I was for them'. Caring for their special needs brought her out of herself; she has driven the community bus and presented programs on community radio. But she never wanted to stand out from the crowd; the trick was to make the special seem ordinary.

*

This book has charted the course of adoption in Australia over the last two centuries. It began as an informal response by family and neighbours to the needs of children whose parents could not care from them. As cities grew adoption became a trade between strangers, with parents and government agents seeking to place children with families who had resources to care for them and need for their love or their labour. When laws were passed in the early twentieth century to regulate this trade they were largely driven by market demand, establishing an exchange which increasingly privileged those wanting to adopt, and denied the rights of birth parents and adoptees. It was not until the 1980s that protests by mothers separated by adoption and their adult children persuaded social workers and politicians to rethink the purpose of adoption—to make it again a service for children in need rather than a service for families wanting children. The open adoption regime which Helen experienced was the result of this rethinking.

This account has been shaped by the circumstances surrounding its making. Written during the years leading up to the national apology, it reflects the voices of those for whom adoption has meant pain and suffering. In the current storm of criticism it has been hard to hear the voices of those untroubled by their adoption experiences. There is still room for debate about some aspects of the impact of closed adoption on individuals and families in Australia. But the truth of the national apology is inescapable: 'We recognise that the consequences of forced adoption practices continue to resonate [painfully] through many, many lives'.

This does not deny that there is still need for some form of adoption. When families fail there can be no doubt that their children need to be cared for in a permanent and secure family environment. The Victorian system of permanent care seems to offer stability without loss of personal identity and contact with family, making it a viable alternative to adoption. But Helen's story shows that like any form of family life, open placement carries its own contradictions.

Open placement commits the child to remembering that they belong to two families. Helen never intended to stand between the children and their parents. But her aim was to make the children forget that they were different from other children; 'we never talked about being fostered'.

At the end of our interview, Helen got out her photo albums. The smiling children looked, as she said, 'just like any other family'.

FURTHER READING

THE SEARCH FOR FAMILY:
A SOCIAL AND POLITICAL HISTORY
OF ADOPTION IN AUSTRALIA

This book comes out of a national research project investigating the history of adoption in Australia. The project examined the distinctive ways in which adoption has reflected and shaped family ideals within Australian settler society. It sought to bring into history the stories of people whose lives have been changed by adoption, in order to acknowledge that experience and to read it against policy change.

The study set out to fill a gap in the nation's self-understanding by explaining the historical factors driving the changing place, meaning and significance of adoption. This undertaking took on added purpose as successive Australian governments, both state and federal, delivered apologies to children and parents who were victims of past policies of forced removal.

Relevant publications by the authors and other members of the research team are listed below. Those interested in reading more about the history of Australian adoption, primary and secondary, will find a comprehensive listing on the Monash History of Adoption project website at:

http://artsonline.monash.edu.au/historyofadoption/

General

Cuthbert, D. 2010. 'Beyond Apologies: Historical Reflections on Policy and Practice Relating to the Out-of-home Care of Children in Contemporary Australia'. *Children Australia*, 35(2): 12–17.

Cuthbert, D., Murphy K., Quartly, M. 2009. 'Adoption and Feminism: Towards Framing a Feminist Response to Contemporary Developments in Adoption'. *Australian Feminist Studies* 24, issue 62: 395–419.

Cuthbert, D., Quartly, M. (eds). 2010. *Adoption, Fostering, Permanent Care and Beyond: Re-Thinking Policy and Practice in Out-of-home Care for Children in Australia.* Special issue of *Children Australia*, 35(2).

Cuthbert, D., Quartly, M. 2012. '"Forced Adoption" in the Australian Story of National Regret and Apology'. *Australian Journal of Politics and History* 58: 82–96.

Cuthbert, D., Quartly, M. 2013. 'Forced Child Removal and the Politics of National Apologies in Australia'. *American Indian Quarterly* 37(1–2) (Winter-Spring): 178–202.

Howe, R, Swain, S. 1993. *The Challenge of the City: The Centenary History of Wesley Central Mission.* Melbourne: Hyland House.

Murphy, K., Quartly, M., Cuthbert, D. 2009. '"In the best interests of the child": Mapping the (Re) Emergence of Pro-Adoption Politics in Contemporary Australia'. *Australian Journal of Politics and History*, 55(2): 201–218.

Musgrove N., Swain, S. 2010. 'The "Best Interests of the Child" in Historical Perspective'. *Children Australia* 35(2): 35–37.

Quartly, M. 2010. 'The "Rights of the Child" in global perspective'. *Adoption, Fostering, Children Australia* 35(2): 38–42.

Quartly, M. 2012. '"[W]e find families for children, not children for families": An incident in the long and unhappy history of relations between social workers and adoptive parents.' *Social Policy and Society* 11(3): 415–427.

Quartly, M., Cuthbert, D., Murphy, K., 2009. 'Political Representations of Adoption in Australia, 1996–2007.' *Adoption and Culture* 2: 141–158.

Quartly, M., Cuthbert, D., Swain, S. 2012. 'A Report on the Findings of the Monash History of Adoption Project.' *Australian Journal of Adoption* 6 (12): n. p. (Papers of the 10th Australian Adoption Conference). At http://www.nla.gov.au/openpublish/index.php/aja/article/view/2523/2974

Quartly, M., Swain, S. 2012. 'The Market in Children: Analysing the Language of Adoption in Australia.' *History Australia*, 9(2): 69–89.

Spark, C., Cuthbert, D. 2009. *Other People's Children: Adoption in Australia.* Melbourne: Australian Scholarly Publishing.

Swain, P., Swain, S. 1992. *To Search for Self: The Experience of Access to Adoption Information.* Sydney: Federation Press.

Swain, S. 2010. 'Birth and Death in a New Land'. *History of the Family* 15(1): 25–33.

Swain, S. 2011. 'Adoption, Secrecy and the Spectre of the True Mother in Twentieth-century Australia. *Australian Feminist Studies* 26(68): 193–205.

Swain, S. 2011. 'Failing Families: Echoes of Nineteenth Century Child Rescue Discourse in Contemporary Debates around Child Protection.' In Marie-Louise Kulke and Christian Gutlebon (eds), *Neo-Victorian Families: Gender, Sexual and Cultural Politics*, 71-91. Netherlands: Rodopi.

Swain, S. 2010. 'Australia'. In Brigitte Bechtold and Donna Cooper Graves (eds). *An Encyclopedia of Infanticide*, 24–27. Lewiston: The Edwin Mellen Press.

Swain, S. 2012. 'Market Forces: Defining the Adoptable Child, 1860–1940'. *Social Policy and Society* 11(3): 399–414.

Swain, S. 2012. 'Snapshots from the Long History of Adoption in Australia'. *Australian Journal of Adoption* 6(12): n. pag. (Papers of the 10th Australian Adoption Conference.) At: http://www.nla.gov.au/openpublish/index.php/aja/article/view/2550/2996

Swain, S., Howe, R. 1995. *Single Mothers and Their Children: Disposal, Punishment and Survival in Australia.* Melbourne: Cambridge University Press.

Swain, S., Hillel, M. 2010. *Child, Nation, Race and Empire: Child Rescue Discourse, England, Canada and Australia,* 1850–1915. Manchester: Manchester University Press.

Studies of Indigenous Adoption

Cuthbert, D. 2001. 'Holding the Baby: Questions Arising from Research into the Experiences of Non-Aboriginal Adoptive and Foster Mothers of Aboriginal Children'. *Journal of Australian Studies* 22 (59): 39–52.

Cuthbert, D. 2001. 'Stolen Children, Invisible Mothers and Unspeakable Stories: The Experiences of Non-Aboriginal Adoptive and Foster Mothers of Aboriginal Children'. *Social Semiotics* 11(2): 139–154.

Cuthbert, D. 2000. 'Mothering the "Other": Feminism, Colonialism and the Experiences of Non-Adoptive Mothers of Aboriginal Children'. *Balayi: Culture, Law and Colonialism* 1 (1): 31–49.

Swain, S. 2013. '"Homes are Sought for These Children". Locating Adoption within the Australian Stolen Generations Narrative'. *American Indian Quarterly* 37(1–2) (Winter-Spring): 203–217.

Studies of Intercountry Adoption

Cuthbert, D. (ed). 2012. *The Vietnam Inheritance.* Special Issue of *Journal of Australian Studies* 36(4).

Cuthbert, D. (ed). 2012. *Waiting for a Better World: Critical and Interdisciplinary Perspectives on Intercountry Adoption,* Themed section of *Social Policy and Society* 11(3).

Cuthbert, D., Swain, S., Quartly, M. 2010. 'Interdisciplinary Perspectives on Intercountry Adoption in Australia' (Workshop summary). At http://www.assa.edu.au/programs/workshop/workshop.php?id=79

Cuthbert, D., Spark, C., Murphy K. 2010. '"That was then, but this is now". Historical Perspectives on Intercountry and Domestic Child Adoption in Australian Public Policy'. *Journal of Historical Sociology* 23(3): 427–452.

Forkert, J. 2012. 'Refugees, Orphans and a Basket of Cats: The Politics of Operation Babylift'. In Denise Cuthbert (ed), *The Vietnam Inheritance.* Special issue of *Journal of Australian Studies* 36(4): 427–444.

Fronek, P., Cuthbert D. 2012. 'History Repeating... Disaster-Related Intercountry Adoption and the Psychosocial Care of Children'. *Social Policy and Society* 11(3): 429–442.

Fronek, P., Cuthbert, D. 2012. 'The Future of Inter-Country Adoption: A Paradigm Shift for this Century'. *International Journal of Social Welfare* 21(2): 215–224.

Fronek, P., Cuthbert, D. 2013. 'Apologies for Forced Adoption Practices: Implications for Contemporary Intercountry Adoption'. *Australian Social Work.* DOI:10.1080/0312407X.2013.777970.

Murphy, K., Pinto, S., Cuthbert, D. 2010. '"These infants are future Australians": Making the Nation through Intercountry Adoption'. *Journal of Australian Studies* 34(2): 141–161.

Taft, M., Dreyfus, K., Quartly M., Cuthbert., D. Spring 2013. '"I knew who I was not, but not who I was". Public Storytelling in the Lives of Australian Adoptees'. *Oral History* (UK) 41(1): 73–83.

Willing, I., Fronek P., Cuthbert. D. 2012. 'Review of Sociological Literature on Intercountry Adoption'. *Social Policy and Society* 11(3): 465–479.

INDEX